ORNAMENTAL GRASSES
FOR THE SOUTHEAST

PETER LOEWER

Illustrations by Peter Loewer

COOL
SPRINGS
PRESS

Nashville, Tennessee
A Division of Thomas Nelson, Inc.
www.ThomasNelson.com

Photo and Illustration Credits

TABLE OF CONTENTS

"All flesh is grass, and all the goodliness thereof is as the flower of the field . . . "
Isaiah 40:6

I write this preface in the middle of July 2003. As always, our world continues to go through the agonies of perpetual change, and the same holds true for the garden.

Every spring finds new catalogs in the mail, catalogs that offer the biggest and best blooms yet; the most phenomenal vegetables; the most fanciful variegations of leaf, many of which are quite beautiful and many that border on the bizarre. And the "box stores" bring forth a few new items but usually adhere to the tried and true, while the nurseries try to interest a frenzied public in the newest of the new while still championing the best of the old!

Out in the garden the plants continue to grow, continue to flower, continue to confront the pollinators (be they insect, animal, or the wind), continue to seed, and persevere for yet another season.

As in the past, I owe a debt of gratitude to my agent, Dominick Abel; my wife, Jean, for her continued mental encouragement and her physical help in the garden (which grows larger every year); and my best garden friend, Peter Gentling, who knows the ups and downs of the plant world better than most. Then on to new friends: Jenny Andrews, my editor at Cool Springs Press; my North Carolina garden connection, Pam Beck, who's there with friendship and camera; and finally John Greenlee, for his aid and direction through the world of grasses.

Peter Loewer
Asheville, North Carolina

I began my gardening career by working in the backyard for my mother, a woman who found time to raise a family, volunteer for war work during World War II, cook before the days of TV dinners, clean without a maid, wash clothes in an old-fashioned washing machine, and even iron shirts.

She loved gardens and gardening, as did my father and my grandfather. She was delighted that I wished to carry on the gardening tradition and especially pleased when as a fledgling artist—after a brief stint as an abstract impressionist—I turned to botanical illustration as a specialty.

When thinking about botanical art I asked myself which one picture in the entire history of art meant more to me than any other (it's still an image featured in my lectures on ornamental grasses in addition to talks on botanical art).

My answer would be Albrecht Dürer's marvelous watercolor *Das Grosse Rasenstück* (*The Great Piece of Turf*), painted in 1503. Consisting of watercolor and gouache on paper, this great work measures sixteen and one-eighth inches by twelve and five-eighths inches. Among the daisies (*Bellis perennis*), the greater plantain (*Plantago major*), the germander speedwell (*Veronica chamaedrys*), and the dandelion (*Taraxacum officinale*) are smooth meadow-grasses (*Poa pratensis*), creeping bent grass (*Agrostis stolonifera*), and cock's foot grass (*Dactylis glomerata*).

Das Grosse Rasenstück by Albrecht Dürer

If asked about this watercolor most people would comment on the weeds. But others would see what Goethe's young hero, Werther, saw when he commented: "When I lie in the tall grass and, closer thus to the earth, become conscious of the thousand varieties of little plants; when I feel the swarming of all that diminutive world amongst the blades . . . I say to myself: 'Ah! If you could but express, if you could but bring to live again on paper, the feeling that pulses so richly, so warmly within you, so that it might become the mirror of your soul . . .'"

Illustration of grasses from *Einzug der Gräser und Farne in die Gärten* by Karl Foerster.

There's a book, too, that inspired me. It's *Einzug der Gräser und Farne in die Gärten* by Karl Foerster (1874–1970), a fantastic volume devoted to the study of ornamental grasses by the man who was the first—and who has done more than any other—to promote their use. The pictures are poor quality black and white with just a few in color (including *Festuca glauca* and *Molinia altissima*); my copy was published in 1957, just twelve years after the war. But they were still identifiable thanks to the use of scientific names, and those photos were enough to fire up the imagination of a gardener.

And, amazingly enough, many of the popular grasses of today are found in precise descriptions in that volume.

This book deals with a very small segment of the more than ten thousand catalogued species: the grasses grown for ornament in home and garden. I hope that you, the reader, find them as fascinating, as interesting, and as beautiful as I do.

THE BOTANY OF GRASSES

Only a few places on this earth immediately tell the viewer about the beauty of the grasses, much less the economic importance. One is a Midwestern cornfield, stretching on to the far horizon, leaves rustling in the wind and tassels waving back and forth under a blazing sun and a blue, blue sky. Another is the vibrant green of the grasses that carpet the earth of the Irish or English coastlines, a green so grand that poets have written about its beauty. The third could be the tall grasses of the American prairies, again moving in the wind as if they were an inland sea. Then there are the rice fields of Asia, broad plains of wet meadows, filled with row upon row of lush green plants that provide the food for nations. And just to salute the mundane, let's mention the fertilized and well-tended grasses of a championship golf course.

All these plants mention-ed are members of the Graminae (or sometimes referred to as the Poaceae), the single most important plant family on earth. They alone produce all the cereal grains that have sustained humanity throughout history. Grasses are responsible for

A garden of diverse grasses.

wheat that produces flour; corn for cereal grain; rice as a basic food staple; the flavorful grains of oats, barley, and rye; the sorghums, responsible for molasses; and cane sugar, feeding the sweet tooth of the world. These plants, and many others, store in their seeds and foliage the vitamins, starches, and sugars that can feed the world.

In addition, grasses produce an amazing number of valuable by-products, including fibers that produce cloth and paper, aromatic oils (that lemony smell in your detergent comes from tropical lemon grass, not from lemons), glues and adhesives, and alcohol. And let's not overlook the roots of grasses, so valuable in preventing erosion on hills or riverbanks or holding great lands in place, like Florida's everglades.

Hundreds of grass species are at home in America and many other species have been introduced from the dirt used for ballast in early ships, seeds mixed into various packing materials, stowaways in grain ship-ments, or stuck to imported wools or the shoes and clothing of passengers returning from other shores. This book deals with grasses

9

grown as ornament and covers a very small segment of the more than ten thousand catalogued species of grasses represented in some seven hundred genera.

Papyrus has been used to make paper since ancient times.

The ornamental grasses have been popular in Europe and Asia for hundreds of years but, except for a period of heightened interest during the years roughly referred to as the American Victorian period, American gardeners have passed them by. Back in the 1950s and 1960s, if the American public knew grasses at all, it was as dried additions to winter bouquets or as a term for marijuana.

There are, perhaps, more than a few reasons for this oversight. Most of the world's other cultures still maintain some contact with the land, and the concept of gardening—whether as food for the body or the soul—has a long and well-documented tradition.

I have a book on floral engravings, originally printed in 1696, showing feather grass (then called *Gramen Plumeum* and now known as *Stipa pennata*) as a decorative garden

addition in Holland. Today, in England and Europe, most of the population garden in one way or another, from window boxes to pot gardens, from allotment gardening to grand estates. Houseplants have been in vogue since the invention of the first "orangeries" or greenhouses in Jane Austin's time. Remember that life in a European coal or industrial town was at best drab and dismal, and people naturally turned to plants to bring a little bit of color into their lives. This long history of exposure to plants has led to a greater sophistication on the part of the European gardener.

Initially, here in America only the landed gentry had gardens for pleasure, as opposed to the farmers who never had time for most ornamental horticulture. It was only with the

Wild grasses potted up for a terrace garden.

Blue fescue can be enjoyed for its color, texture, and form.

rising middle class that gardens became a natural addition to many, but not all, homes.

In Japan and China, where gardens have been appreciated for thousands of years, it's no longer important how many plant varieties one can grow, but rather how many qualities one can find in a single plant. Theirs is a culture that finds restful contemplation in gardens made entirely of mosses, grasses, or stones; not only does a gardener enjoy a flower, but the stem, the leaf, the entire plant, and even the shadow it casts upon a garden wall.

Today, our culture is a mobile one, and because of economic and professional demands the typical family no longer settles in one place for its entire existence. Patience is a rare commodity and few people bother with the less

flamboyant or slower-growing members of the plant world. Instead, they demand the fast tree and the blatant bloom, and thus many of the grasses are left to the lawn for cutting and the gift shops in the local mall as dried flowers, where they remind us of our agricultural past.

At this point I'm reminded of an old story (probably apocryphal) of two American visitors to a grand English estate.

"Goodness," said the wife as she trod the palatial lawn, "this grass is beautiful." Then turning to the head gardener, she asked: "How do you get a beautiful lawn like this?"

"Well," he replied, "first you roll it for about four hundred years."

The Concise Oxford Dictionary: Fifth Edition defines the word grass as "Herbage of which blades or leaves and stalks are eaten by cattle, horses, sheep, etc. . . . any species of this (including in botanical use, excluding in popular use) the cereals, reeds, and bamboos . . ." This is probably as good a definition as any other.

For references to grass that are further afield, we have the following: "Never let the grass grow under one's feet;" "snake in the grass;" "a grass widow" (referring to the actual state of widowhood); "turn out to grass" (another way of saying "put out to pasture," which is a deplorable habit of American civilization); "Go to grass!" (a polite way of

A real snake in the grass.

telling somebody off); "keep off the grass;" "grass doesn't grow on a busy street;" "a grass colt" (referring to a colt with unknown parentage—and a slang way of saying the same about people); "bring to grass" (an English term that refers to shooting an animal or bird); and finally the term made so popular during the 1960s—"smoking grass."

In the United States, the grasses are represented by more than 1,400 naturally occurring species. Grasses run the gamut from the 120-foot giant bamboo (*Dendrocalamus giganteus*) to the tiny dwarf fescues (*Festuca* spp.), only a few inches high. We're all familiar with food grasses, but most domestic animals and many in the wild depend on the forage grasses that produce hay, the pasture grasses best represented by little bluestem (*Schizachyrium scoparium*), the big bluestem (*Andropodon gerardi*), and the silage grasses such as corn and sorghum.

One of the small fountain grasses.

Grasses are also used to fight erosion. Vast stretches of American beaches have been planted with American beach grass (*Ammophila breviligulata*) and sea oats (*Chasmanthium latifolium*) because their tight,

fibrous root systems dig in and keep sand from blowing away. Cord grass (*Spartina* spp.) and reed (*Phragmites* spp.) perform the same service for many of the coastal wetlands and shallow marshes. In fact, if it wasn't for the latter species, New Jersey might float out to sea.

Grasses can be found even in unused, inhospitable places.

Bamboos are grasses, too, and used all over the Orient for construction scaffolding, water pipes, cooking utensils, food, art objects, and decorative garden and house plants.

Besides lichens and algae, the grasses are the only other plants found in the remote polar regions and the hottest deserts of the world. The next time you pass a construction site, where the worst soil imaginable has been piled up next to stagnant pools of water, chances are you'll find a few grasses starting to reach for the sky above. Their ability to withstand prolonged periods of drought, to form extensive mats of growth (because of their habit of rooting along their stems at the swollen joints called nodes), their dependence on wind rather than insects for pollination, and very efficient seed production and great methods of dispersal have given the grasses an A+ grade on the evolutionary report and a greater range around the world than any other plant family.

A Word About Nomenclature

In his 1983 book *Botanical Latin*, Dr. William Stearn, the senior principal scientific officer of the Department of Botany at the British Museum, described botanical Latin as " . . . a modern Romance language of special technical application, derived from Renaissance Latin with much plundering of ancient Greek, which has evolved, mainly since 1700 and primarily through the work of Carl Linnaeus (1707–1778), to serve as an international medium for the scientific naming of plants in all their vast numbers and manifold diversity. These include many thousands of plants unknown to the Greeks and Romans of classical times and for which names have had to be provided as a means of reference."

Scientific Latin is a universal language. Every plant species has its own unique name.

Regardless of what language the collector or the gardener speaks, the scientific name of the plant he or she is working with remains inviolate throughout the world. Although it's true that many grasses can be recognized by

their common names, many others cannot. So gardeners will note that most catalogs (if not all), provide both the common name and the scientific name for the plants they sell.

Many terms are in use, but for gardeners four serve for identification purposes: genus, species, variety, and cultivar. All reference books, most gardening books, nearly all responsible catalogs and nurseries, and even the majority of seed packets list the scientific name along with the common. In many cases, the common names of popular plants are also their scientific names, and people use them every day without realizing it. Delphinium, geranium, sedum, and gladiolus come to mind.

Plants with similar forms might be unrelated. Liriope (left) is in the family Liliaceae and sedges (right) are in the family Cyperaceae.

Genus refers to a group of plants that are closely related, while species suggests an individual plant's unique quality, color, or even habit of growth. Either genus or species names may honor the person who discovered the plant. For example, the spiderworts are called *Tradescantia* after John Tradescant, one of the greatest and most adventurous of the English plant collectors.

Genus and species names can also be descriptive. The genus of the annual grass

13

Muhlenbergia dumosa, named for botanist G.H.E. Muhlenberg, sometimes called the American Linnaeus.

the abbreviation "var."—which is not italicized. The genus is capitalized while the species is set in lower case. Genus, species, and variety names are italicized or underlined, unless the general text is set in italics, in which case the scientific name is not italicized.

The fourth term, cultivar, was introduced in 1923 by famous botanist and horticulturist Liberty Hyde Bailey, and derived from the words "**culti**vated **vari**ety." A cultivar represents a desirable variation that appears on a plant that is in cultivation, and could result from either chance or design. The cultivar is set off by single quotation marks. The variegated form of the grass miscanthus is thus *Miscanthus sinensis* 'Variegatus'.

Miscanthus sinensis 'Variegatus' is a cultivated variety of maiden grass.

golden top is *Lamarkia*, named for the French naturalist J. B. Lamarck, while its species is *aurea*, from a Latin word for yellow.

The third term, variety, is often abbreviated to "var." A variety represents a noticeable change in a plant's form that develops by chance in nature and breeds true from generation to generation. The variegated variety of Simon's bamboo is *Arundinaria simonii* var. *variegata*. When used, the variety name is also italicized and usually preceded by

Many plants listed in catalogs have scientific names that are woefully out of date. This is because the catalog writers know that the public recognizes the older names, but rarely knows the new.

The Anatomy of Grass
The **stems**—or as they are correctly called—**culms** (1) of grasses are usually round and hollow, as in wheat, but sometimes have solid stems as in corn. These stem sections are

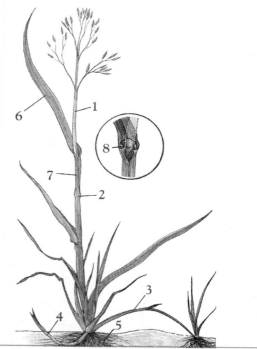

Parts of a grass.

grass without a good deal of hard digging. The great prairies of America were once covered with vast areas of grasses that would burn from lightning strikes, producing awesome prairie fires. Yet, because the deep roots were never even singed, new grass would grow again the following spring. These roots also saved many Midwest grasses from damage by drought.

Grass leaves are always parallel-veined and belong to that great group of plants known as the monocotyledons, easily identified by seedlings that always begin with one leaf, not two. These leaves consist of a **blade** (6) and a **sheath** (7) that surrounds the culm. Where the blade meets the sheath, a small hairy collar is usually found. This is called the **ligule** (8), which means "little tongue," and is a distinguishing characteristic of grasses.

Because most of the grasses depend on the wind for pollination, they have no need for large and brilliant floral displays, those garish petals necessary to attract bees,

joined by solid **joints** or **nodes** (2). Such stems stand erect, like the grasses found in those great fields of wheat or corn; bend at the joints like many of the panic grasses; or trail along the soil surface like crab grass, in which case the stems are known as **stolons** (3).

When the stolons continue to grow just beneath the ground's surface, they are called **rhizomes** (4), and the growth of these rhizomes is a great method of reproduction, almost as effective as seeds, amply demonstrated by the ability of your lawn grasses to spread.

Grass root systems are very **fibrous** (5) and many types of grass have roots that penetrate the earth for many feet, often straight down. It's this quality that makes the grasses so valuable in erosion control and also prevents you from completely removing an unwanted

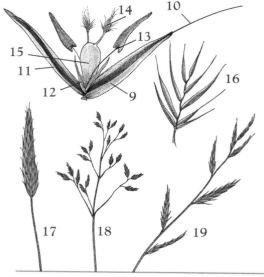

Parts of grass flowers and forms of spikelets.

butterflies, moths, ants, beetles, and birds to move pollen about to ensure pollination and seed formation.

The grasses cast their pollen out to float from flower to flower on gentle breezes. Their flower parts are essentially the same as other flowering plants, but a few of the features, such as petals, have all but disappeared. The rest are so small that a magnifying glass is necessary to see them. The **lemma** (9), which in turn gives rise to another major feature of the grasses, the **awn** (10); the **palea** (11); and the **lodicule** (12) are but the remains of the petals of a typical flower. The **stamens** (13) are male and the **stigma** (14)—usually plumed to aid in picking pollen out of the air—is female and surmounts the **ovary** (15), where the seeds are produced.

The flower cluster (or the inflorescence) is made up of subdivisions called **spikelets** (16) and are usually perfect, meaning both male and female parts are found within the same bloom. The spikelets are arranged in three different forms: **terminal spikes** (17) as in foxtail grass, a **panicle** as in orchard grass (18), and a **raceme** as in the common manna grasses (19).

Many grasses flower with such precise timing that a watch (or at least a sundial) could be set by their blooming habits. The *Briza* species open at about 6:00 a.m., while most of the brome grasses bloom at 2:00 p.m., and the *Avena* species begin around 3:00 p.m. The process begins when the lemma and palea start to open, allowing the anthers to spread and shake their pollen into the wind. On another grass, feathery stigmas are now ready to receive pollen from other flowers. Grasses rarely self-fertilize as they are usually sterile to their own pollen.

Seeds of Grasses

The seeds of the grasses assume many shapes and sizes, all readily adapted to dispersal by the wind and animals, including man. Many grass seeds have sharp awns that can pierce an animal's skin or become entangled in its fur, and thus travel for miles before the seed falls to the earth and germinates. The twisted portion of the awn found in porcupine grass (*Stipa spartea*) coils and uncoils as the moisture content of the air changes, causing the bent arm of the awn to revolve slowly until it touches grass stems or other objects. Then the

Pennisetum setaceum 'Rubrum' is perennial in Zone 9, but annual in cooler regions.

entire seed is literally screwed into the earth. Unfortunately, the same process occurs if the florets lodge in the wool or hair of animals, often causing serious puncture wounds to grazing animals. Needle grass (*Aristida oligatha*) and squirrel's-tail grass (*Hordeum jubatum*) do the same.

Other grass seeds are less harmful, exhibiting long and attractive plumes that float them through the air like dandelion fluff.

Man, too, has been an active agent in the spread of grasses. Many African species that were used to stuff bedding in slave ships, such as Bermuda grass and molasses grass, followed along and began to grow in waste areas around various ports-of-call. Canary grass, as noted in the chapter on annual grasses, often escapes from the birdcage bottom and is found growing at the town dump.

Finally, grass seeds have frequently come into the country as impurities in other seed mixes or even in grain shipments.

How Grasses Grow

With some exceptions, grasses belong to three major groups: annuals, biennials, and perennials. Annual grasses such as hare's-tail grass will germinate, grow from seedlings into adult plants, flower, then set seed, all in one year and often in one season.

Biennial grasses germinate in one season, grow, then overwinter, continuing to grow into the next year, when they flower, then die.

Perennial grasses live and grow for more than two seasons and many perennial grasses will persist in the garden for years. Sometimes, depending on the conditions in a region, a species of grass can be an annual, a biennial, or a short-lived perennial.

Grasses also fall into two categories usually regulated by climate: warm-season grasses and cool-season grasses.

Warm-season grasses are usually dormant until temperatures warm up in spring. They grace our gardens during the summer months, performing best at temperatures between 80°F and 95°F. They flower and go to seed toward the end of the growing season, turn marvelous colors in the fall, then become dormant for the worst of the winter, with leaves often turning white. Some of these grasses will be beautiful all winter long, standing up to wind, rain, and occasional snow, while others eventually become victims of the weather, looking shabby at best.

Warm-season grasses like *Miscanthus* often have beautiful fall colors.

17

Cool-season grasses dislike hot weather and begin to show signs of life in late winter or early spring. They prefer temperatures of 60°F to 75°F, flower early, and either stop growing completely or slow down a great deal during the hot summer months.

Habit of Growth

Ornamental grasses usually exhibit two methods of growth: running and clumping. Running grasses are best exemplified by your lawn, lawn invaders such as crabgrass, and many of the bamboos. Clumping grasses grow as tight, generally circular mounds that increase in diameter every new season, and eventually form centers of dead culms or stems. Some clumpers are also spreaders, but they are in a minority.

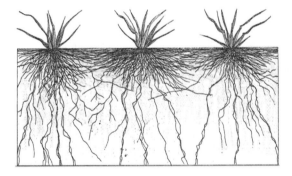

The arching form of a *Stipa*.

Grass Forms

Finally, ornamental grasses that form clumps are usually found growing in one of the following shapes: upright, mounded, fountain-like, upright-divergent, tufted, arching, or trailing.

Forms of grasses: upright, mounded, fountain-like, upright-divergent, tufted, arching, and trailing.

DESIGNING WITH GRASSES

Texture, Movement, and Patterns of Light

Much of the beauty found in grasses stems from (if you'll excuse the pun) the reaction of the leaves to the slightest wind, and the sound the rustling leaves make in the summer and the stiffer sound heard in winter. Then, as the light filters through layers of foliage, highlights and shadows become abstract paintings, only to change their moods when hit by rain or pellets of ice, or gracefully bent under the weight of a rare snowfall. The light tan and reddish buff colors of winter grasses stand out against a dark winter sky and bring the type of drama to gardens that most perennials only begin to provide. Plumes rise in the air, plumes that could grace Cleopatra's barge floating down the River Nile. In striking contrast to the damage it can do to other plants, wind actually benefits a garden with grasses.

When used in great concentrations, the grasses bend to the wind and become a minor "Sea of Grass" in your own backyard. Planted in water gardens, grasses not only help stabilize the edge of a flowing creek or a small pond, their reflections in still

Backlit *Miscanthus* seedheads.

or moving water become abstract sculptures moving in and out to the rhythm of the wind. All the wonderful and graceful sedges, the spiked stems of the rushes, the sausage tops of the cattails, and the stiff leaves of the various *Acorus* species bring even more delight to your design.

Finally, when a light snow blankets the garden, the dried leaves and stems of the grasses—plus the still-remaining seedpods—become beautifully etched lines on a white paper made of ice.

The Design Quality of the Grasses

Russell Page, the great garden and landscape designer (1906–1985), installed a marvelous garden full of grasses on the grounds of Pepsi-Cola's corporate headquarters in Purchase, New York. Critics thought that a garden of grasses would eventually be boring, but it isn't, and it won't ever be unless the wind stops blowing and the rain and snow stop falling.

To enhance the design aspects, Page installed islands of various grasses surrounded by a cut lawn, with the lawn forming a frame for the various groupings. He worked with clumping grasses because, while becoming larger every growing season, they do stay in one place. Page used maiden grasses (*Miscanthus* 'Gracillimus') to fill large islands of the garden, along with various blue fescues (*Festuca* spp.), and *Molinia caerulea* cultivars such as 'Windspiel' and 'Skyracer'.

Wild sedges in a backyard pool.

Little bluestem in a snowstorm.

Russell Page grass garden at Pepsico.

In the chapter on perennial grasses, you'll find that color variations number in the hundreds, not to mention the different textures. Some grasses have thin, spike-like leaves, while others have blades that wrap about stiff stems for many feet before arching out like stiff ribbons with trimmed tips. In many cases the denuded culms become a design element on their own—by removing browned leaves from the stems of most miscanthus, you can create a dramatic element in the garden, with fresh green leaves on top and bamboo-like stems below.

Imagine a small chessboard with four rows of squares instead of eight, with one blue oat grass (*Helictotrichon sempervirens*) planted at each corner and various sedums between them. Now imagine a food mall in Hamilton, Ohio, where I saw the median between a divided highway planted with horsetails (*Equisetum hyemale*), a tough, resilient plant resembling long green pencils circled here and there with rings of black-bordered tan.

The sky is literally the limit when it comes to designing with grasses.

Stems of eulalia grass are a design element on their own.

Using Grasses As Specimen Plants

Few perennial plants make the architectural statement that a large ornamental grass can achieve when set in a place of honor. Such clumps of grasses, ranging from the commonplace to the rare, can be as striking as a piece of outdoor sculpture—plus the grasses can move with the breeze.

Many of the large grasses have a monumental quality that often fights with other plants, including bushes and small trees, unless the grasses are isolated against a background of the sky or a beautiful old garden wall. And when up-lit with some outdoor lights, they excite from morning to night.

Right now out on our sunlit terrace, I have some great pots that I've collected from flea markets and garage sales, and each one is host to a great ornamental grass. They range from a muhly grass (*Muhlenbergia dumosa*) to lemon

Zebra grass makes a stunning backdrop in a mountain garden.

grass (*Cymbopogon citratus*) to the new purple millet (*Pennisetum glaucum* 'Purple Majesty'). The muhly grass is planted in a large, black, rounded Mexican pottery container, while the lemon grass rises from a piece of contemporary pottery with a light brown glaze. The millet shoots up from another contemporary pot, this one with a purple glaze with silver splashes around the edge. Each is a stunning addition to any collection of specimen plants.

Then out in the garden proper, in what has turned into a place of honor, sits the three-year-old hardy Chinese sugar cane (*Saccharum arundinaceum*), this July morning standing tall at ten feet with another three months of growth ahead.

Mixing Grasses with Other Perennials

I present a lecture dealing with designing small gardens. In one section I talk about using a plant as a garden focal point, usually suggesting a plant that has interest for at least three seasons of the year.

A case in point would be a perennial bed planted with various low grasses, blooming annuals, and bright perennials, but with a centerpiece of purple moor grass (*Molinia caerulea* 'Variegata') or perhaps the dwarf form of Pampas grass (*Cortaderia selloana* 'Pumila'), instead of a gazing globe or a birdbath.

In the spring, attention is shared between the usual run of flowers and the fresh new leaves of the grass. Then as late spring and early summer flowers begin to fade, the plumes of the grasses appear, providing their share of visual interest until frost enters the scene in mid-autumn. Then as the plumes get larger and often shed their seed, the leaves of the grasses turn all shades of brown and tan, usually with highlights of red, russet, and orange.

In our lakeside garden we grow a large zebra grass behind a clump of one of our showiest native

Cymbopogon citratus in a decorative pot.

flowers, the fire red blossoms of *Hibiscus coccineus*, bunched together on top of six- to seven-foot stems, the flowers backed by the stripes of the grass.

Or you could mix *Miscanthus* 'Cabaret' with one of the hydrangeas, such as *Hydrangea paniculata* 'Limelight', with the cool green flowers blooming from midsummer into autumn, seen through the arching variegations of the grass.

Growing Grasses for Their Flowers

When it comes to flowers, the grass family shines its brightest. Because grasses depend on the wind for pollination, they have no use for large and gaudy floral displays, where colorful petals and sweet nectars work together to attract bees, wasps, ants, beetles, and birds to complete the job of pollination. Instead, the

Even a shade garden can include grasses and sedges.

Molinia in spring, summer, and fall.

designed by nature to pick pollen grains right out of the air. Below the stigmas are large stamens with anthers at their tips; these manufacture the pollen grains that contribute half of the genes necessary for seed formation.

Because of their dependence on the wind, most of the ripening seedheads are open to the air, rather than being enclosed in a fruit (to be eaten) or a capsule (to split open and spill heavy seeds directly on the ground). The seedheads of grasses are usually light and fluffy, beautiful in the garden when fresh, sprinkled with raindrops, or covered with the dews of morning. Then when

Stipa tenuissima seedheads bring texture and movement to a garden.

grasses simply let the wind carry male pollen to the female receptors, and seedpods form.

Usually both male and female parts are found within the same blossom. The female ovary is topped with plumed stigmas especially

they dry, their colors change, and most look beautiful throughout the winter, until weather takes its toll and they shatter.

Nature makes sure that each grass plant produces enough seeds for the survival of the species. Every grass bears many individual flowers that are gathered together in clusters, or inflorescences. The flower clusters consist of spikelets arranged in three different forms: panicles as found in the eulalia grasses (*Miscanthus* spp.); racemes as seen in the open and airy flowers of a plant such as Natal grass (*Rhynchelytrum repens*); and spikes, seen in the seedheads of grasses such as fountain grass (*Pennisetum* spp.).

Fountain grasses in bloom.

For the most exceptional floral characteristics of all, remember to look at (and be sure to grow) the flower heads produced by the annual grasses. Here nature's imagination ranges from the heavy-laden foxtail grasses to the delicate plumes called hare's-tails, named so because that's exactly what they look like.

Grasses As Transitions Between Garden Areas

The tall and grand grasses, plants such as most of the miscanthus tribe or the Pampas grasses, are often used to create living walls or divisions in the landscape. Thanks to their size, they are most effective when used to build living garden walls for separating different garden "rooms."

Or use grasses to bridge the gap between various tree plantings or as transition areas between the plants in the relatively low perennial garden and the woods beyond.

A line of grasses, such as a row of various fescues, becomes a great way to edge a garden walkway or encircle a pond. Think about designing a Brazilian walkway, a sinuous salute to the Carnival in Rio, by planting an

Garden pathway edged with grasses, daisies, and daylilies.

24

assortment of fescues in straight or curving lines along a sidewalk or pathway.

Grasses for Wildlife

Dozens of native perennial grasses are attractive enough to be great ornamentals and their flower heads provide an incredible variety of seeds: broomsedge bluestem (*Andropogon virginicus*), buffalo grass (*Buchloë dactyloides*), river oats (*Chasmanthium latifolium*), June grass (*Koeleria cristata*), switch grass (*Panicum virgatum*), and Indian grass (*Sorghastrum nutans*).

Then there are the annuals such as love grass (*Eragrostis tef*), attractive enough to be eaten by both animals and people; canary grass (*Phalaris canariensis*), so called because it's used as commercial canary food; and the pendant spikes of thousands of seeds, known as the foxtail grasses (*Setaria* spp.). Black sorghum (*Sorghum bicolor* var. *technicus*) has a seed panicle up to a foot long and packed with nutritious seeds. And let's not forget all the wheats, their seeds again prized by birds and the source of our breads and pastas.

Naturalizing Grasses in a Meadow

Gardening, as with anything else, has its vogues. Fashion is not limited to food and

Miss Jekyll, the garden cat.

Stipa in a natural planting.

clothes, although gardeners like to think they are beyond such short-lived fads. For years the vast majority of people cared not a whit about flower gardens or wildflowers, except those few folks classified as conservationists. During the 1970s conservation became popular and on country weekends away from the cities, people discovered both the beauties and physical rewards of gardening. Finally in the 1980s and 1990s, gardening became a trendy avocation, with people vying with each other over unusual garden styles.

One such fashion is the English meadow garden, first discussed in the late 1800s by William Robinson, who suggested planting hardy bulbs in meadow grass—here in Asheville we have naturalized autumn crocus (*Colchicum* spp.) in the lawn. The idea hit the arts and leisure sections of the major newspapers. At the same time, camping and hiking equipment companies featured products such as Meadow-in-a-Can and Monet's Garden in upscale mail-order catalogs. Their colorful ads suggested to readers that vast sweeps of garden color could be theirs with a minimum of work over a short time.

Well, it's a lot harder to establish such gardens than just opening up a can and sprinkling seeds on the ground—as you soon discover by reading the small print on those can labels. But even acknowledging the hard work that's needed to create such gardens, upon completion you'll agree the effort is worth it.

And what does a meadow look like? In early summer, under a clear blue sky, drive along a two-lane country road lined on either side with fields (in a county whose highway department doesn't use defoliants to rid the shoulder of what they love to call "weeds"), and you'll get an idea. A meadow garden is tall, with green grasses swaying in the wind, here and there dotted with daisies and buttercups, with butterflies flying about as if they're in a Disney film.

A meadow garden is not for everyone, and if you do plan on such a design, make sure your neighbors are ready for the concept. But for a vacation home, a secluded backyard, or almost any rural setting, such a garden is a joy to have.

To achieve a meadow garden there are two approaches: First, you just stop cutting the grass and soon those plants you've been cutting will send up flowers and eventually seeds.

Grasses in a mixed border with shrubs, annuals, perennials, and vines.

Then, thanks to updrafts and downdrafts, more seeds arrive by air, not to mention by birds, and eventually you get a meadow.

The second way is to contact your local Extension agent, get a list of appropriate grasses for your area of the Southeast, prepare the site by scarifying the earth and removing as many weeds as possible, then planting them in the same way you would a lawn.

Cloud-Cutting

If you are lucky enough to have meadows surrounding your home but are tired of mowing the whole works every fall, try the concept of cloud-cutting. It requires thinking in grandiose terms, but it saves a great deal of effort in the long run. Between the front of your meadow and your existing lawn, cut the last swath of lawn in graceful curves like the edges of clouds. In the fall of the first year, cut only the front third of the meadow. The second year cut two-thirds of the meadow. Finally, every third year cut the entire meadow.

The result is that the third of the meadow closest to the house changes the most. But the other parts, when allowed to mature, are open to all sorts of different grasses and field flowers from seeds brought in by winds and birds. In fact, in the Southeast, you're never sure just what you'll find. And leaving parts of the meadow undisturbed for periods of time is an invitation to birds and insects that choose to spend the summer near your home. This method of cutting looks especially fine when the meadow is on a gentle hill.

Drying Grasses

Many gardeners who have started a love affair with ornamental grasses soon find that with many of the leaves and dozens of blossoms they have artistic winners in their gardens. Several

26

grass fanciers I know make a bit of pocket money by raising grasses in their cutting gardens, not to mention selling an odd grass or two at various flea markets.

Decorating the home and office with dried grasses is an old, old practice that usually leads to notable additions to indoor ambience. But allow me to warn the reader, that having spent many years with the true colors of nature, I have no patience with the art of dyeing plants, often practiced in up-market shops that should know better.

Centuries ago, the available dyes were of natural origin, produced by living things, mostly plants—give or take an insect or two. Then came the Victorians, who, never to be outdone by nature, developed an array of dyes with brilliant colors based on a new chemistry of coal-tar derivatives. When the Victorian dyes are viewed today in pressed flower paintings or glassed-in bouquets of the period, exposure to light and air over many years has mellowed and muted the colors, but if seen in their pristine intensity, they would knock your eyes out. Remember that they had no bright or fluorescent lights, and kept the sun out with heavy drapes to prevent the fabrics around the room from fading, so the pressure was on to make the colors unnaturally bright. I resent the

River oats make great dried flowers.

artificial colors of today with their vermilions, acid-greens, deep purples, and, to me, worst of all, turquoise spray paints and find them doubly offensive when placed on dried blossoms.

So to learn about dyeing, you must search elsewhere. But if you are interested in the art of drying—that is, drying grasses in their natural majesty—then read on. It's a remarkably simple process: All you need is wire coat hangers, paper twist-ties left over from plastic bags, and a sharp knife or scissors.

Gather the grasses in mid-afternoon on a dry and sunny day, after the dews of morning have evaporated and before the late afternoon damp sets in. Pick stems with blossoms not yet completely open, and cut the stems as long as you can. It's much easier to trim stems for a shorter arrangement than glue stems back together for length.

Strip any excess leaves—which will only shrivel into a sorry state during the drying process—and leave only the seedheads and panicles. Tie small bunches of stems together so that air can pass easily between each stem, and hang them upside down on the coat hangers, again allowing plenty of room between bunches. Then hang the hangers well apart in a basement room or garage that is cool, dry, dark, and airy. The cool temperature prevents the plant sap from drying too quickly and forcing the spikelets to go to seed; the dry and airy atmosphere prevents the formation of mold and mildew; and the darkness prevents premature fading of the floral parts.

Check your bundles every few days to be sure they are securely tied, because as the stems dry they also shrink and could fall to the floor and be ruined.

Most of the straight grasses should be dried this way. Seedheads such as the foxtails, which benefit from a curved stem, should be staked in a dry vase or container, and kept upright but stored in the same safe place.

Cattails are always easy to dry if you pick them while the male flowers—the pollen-laden spikes on top of the tail—are still in bloom. Stand the stalks in a narrow can or jar so that they dry in an upright position. If picked too late, the cattails will turn into an expanding mass of airborne seeds with attached fluff, which will travel all over the house.

The delicate flower heads of muhly grass.

Many of the leaves of grasses, especially the reeds and the cultivars of the eulalias, are excellent additions to dried arrangements.

For grasses with delicate seedheads, such as cloud grass and champagne grass, a very light coating of hairspray is often helpful for holding it all together.

Several grasses with dried leaves will release pleasant fragrances into the air. Especially fragrant are lemon grass (*Cymbopogon citratus*), sweet vernal grass (*Anthoxanthum odoratum*), and khus-khus (*Vetiveria zizanoides*).

Floral Arrangements

Arranging flowers, whether fresh or dried, is a matter of personal taste, but a few general suggestions might be helpful.

Try to use containers of natural materials, such as stoneware crocks, jugs, and even wicker baskets. In essence you are trying to match textures: Most dried grass arrangements would be out of place in a highly patterned Sèvres porcelain vase.

Think of scale. Ordinarily you would not take five cattails and use them with one piece of cloud grass, as one would completely dominate the other. But if you massed thirty stems of cloud grass together, the visual impact would work harmoniously with the cattails.

The flowers of 'Moudry' fountain grass echo the purple leaves of *Cordyline australis* 'Purple Tower'.

Although their colors are similar, the textures of 'Kaga Nishiki' sedge and 'Butter Pat' coleus are a good contrast.

Avoid the obvious. Driftwood is great on beaches and even has a place in many decorative themes, but unless you come up with a unique way of using it, it will detract from most dried flower arrangements.

Very complicated arrangements should not be pushed into a tight little corner because most such arrangements need a sense of air around them. And dark subjects usually look best against light-colored walls. Finally, don't forget the wonderful effect of light and shadow both on the arrangement and the space behind it.

Grasses in the Wild

One of the stellar things about gardening is discovering the beauty of a wild plant—getting that first glimpse of something that had until then escaped your notice. While many wild plants become too weedy for civilization, with a tendency to overtake the rest of the garden, some wild ones are so beautiful that you might consider planting a wild garden where confusion and chaos is the rule rather than clipped perfection.

A selection of interesting wild grasses are listed below. The numbers refer to the accompanying illustration.

1. *Aristida wrightii*, Wright's triple-awned grass, is a member of the needle grasses and is considered to be dangerous for animals because the sharp awns can easily inflict injury. But if set into a protected area, they excel when cut and dried for winter bouquets.

2. *Bromus inermis*, smooth brome grass, is a perennial sod grass, native to Europe and China. It was introduced to the United States in 1884 and has since been widely grown as a pasture and hay grass. It frequently escapes from cultivation and grows along roadside ditches and on the edges of fields. The stems grow to three to four feet, and the panicles dry to the golden-brown common to most of the bromes.

3. *Bromus secalinus*, wild chess, is another annual and weedy grass. Although it doesn't have the values of most species grown for ornament, it deserves to be used in dried arrangements for its color alone. The chess grasses dry to a rich, golden-brown color that will remind the viewer of summers past.

4. *Dactylis glomerata*, orchard grass, was introduced into the country about 1760 when it came from Europe as a forage grass. First cultivated in Virginia, it's now found almost

everywhere and is still used for hay. The plants grow in large tussocks.

5. *Elymus cillosus*, wild rye, is a perennial found along stream banks and old roads. The leaves are thin and dark, with the upper surface velvety to the touch. Often confused with bottlebrush grass, wild rye is a bit weedy for the garden but fine for dried arrangements.

6. *Holcus lanatus*, velvet grass, once held in high esteem for hay, has now been banished to the weed category. Cattle were never fond of it and in the 1800s, the Duke of Bedford, following the sage suggestion of Sir Humphrey Davy, experimented with sprinkling salt over the hay to make it more palatable. Animals, however, still showed good sense and refused to touch it.

7. *Leersia oryzoides*, cut grass, is named for the margins of the leaf blades, which are covered with sharp little spines that can catch on your skin and clothing and cut your hands. So use caution when gathering. This grass is found on the edge of a swamp or wetland and easily reaches a five-foot height. The panicles, when carefully dried, are beautiful with their shiny black spikelets.

8. *Setaria viridis*, green foxtail grass, looks exactly like its namesake. This common annual grass is a weedy pest to farmers and, after banishment from the field, is often found along the graveled soft shoulder of Southern highways. The green color, unlike many other grasses, remains after drying.

7   8   3   4   6   5   1   2

GROWING AND CARING FOR GRASSES

It's easy to forget that ornamental grasses are annuals and perennials that are grown for their leaves or their blossoms, or both. And just like growing a hosta or a rose, grasses need nearly the same kind of care as other plants.

While many perennial grasses can be grown from seed—and sometimes that's the only way to find a rare or unusual grass—it's often faster (sometimes by two or three years) to buy established plants from nurseries or the rare garden center that has a good collection of grasses. Today, with the competition between the U.S. Postal Service and package delivery services such as UPS, you'll find that plants properly packed will arrive safely at your door—and most nurseries guarantee safe arrival. Just make sure that you choose the proper time for ordering plants, usually very early spring or mid- to late fall, and not the height of the summer when no amount of care and packing will protect a living thing during shipment.

In most of the South only two major chores are connected with growing and maintaining grasses: dividing a large, mature clumper, for example, a species of eulalia grass (*Miscanthus* spp.); and cutting back the previous year's growth.

In areas with mild winters and not too much snow or ice, the dead tops of perennial grasses that have gone dormant last a long time. So it's up to the gardener to decide when he or she is really getting tired of the tattered look of the leaves, and that the time has come for shearing. Remember, get the job done before the new growth is so high that it will be clipped in the process. When most ornamentals are not cut back in time, the new spring growth is delayed and the mix of the new and the old makes the plants look decidedly forlorn.

Usually just a sharp pair of secateurs will do, but for really tough grass clumps, an electric hedge trimmer is useful. Even if permitted, never burn grasses to clear up last year's foliage or you risk damaging the crown.

In early spring, after you have finished cutting back the old growth, you can side-dress the clump with a 12-6-6 fertilizer. If your soil has generally poor quality, fertilize again in midsummer. Mulching always helps, especially to conserve water, but also to keep roots cool and discourage weeds.

Gardener's gators and *Lamium* 'Beacon Silver'.

Planting New Grasses

Grasses are certainly not overly fussy plants and many will make do with a small space carved out of the wilderness. But for grasses to perform their best and delight you and your garden visitors, you should begin by making sure your soil is as good as you can get it.

Most grasses, except those that adapt to wet or boggy conditions, need good drainage. If you garden on solid clay or solid rock, you should probably build a low stone wall or raised beds using chemical-free railroad ties.

If you have the time and energy, you can amend the soil using a small cultivator and adding compost or a commercial soil amender. If you are working the surface soil and find hard soil beneath, poke holes into the ground using a stout metal rod. Over time water will seep into those holes and eventually help to break up the subsoil. I space these holes about six inches apart.

For sandy soil, the trick is to keep it from draining too quickly. Such soil is great for grasses that naturally grow on sand dunes, but prairie grasses need different conditions. Here again, work in compost or other organic matter.

If you are starting work on a new grass bed, this is probably a great time to remove all existing weeds and amend the soil. For an island bed, you can use a garden hose to outline the shape of the bed. Once the outline is in place, you can remove the existing turf—using a flat spade—then proceed to break up the newly exposed dirt. Then amend as suggested earlier. Until the grasses grow and fill out, you can cover the bare earth with mulch, using commercial compost, pine needles, or pine nuggets.

Most ornamental grasses grow best in full to part sun, but they tolerate a wide range of growing conditions. If you are planting them in an existing bed, little improvement will be needed. Turn the soil and then incorporate a two-inch layer of organic matter in the area to be planted.

Break up the bottom of the root ball before you put the grass in the hole. This will help the roots spread out, instead of continuing to grow in a circle after planting. This is especially necessary if the plant is root bound. Fill the bottom of the hole with water, place the grass in the hole, then fill in with soil, pushing it down and around the root ball. Be careful to plant the

Hardy sugar cane stays beautiful into the early winter.

Cut back grasses before new growth appears in spring.

Most grasses, such as this *Miscanthus* (left), need good drainage.

ornamental grass at the same level it was growing in the container. Many plants die from crown rot because they were planted too deep.

After planting, watch and water the plant as needed. Do not let the grasses wilt or dry out too much, as it weakens the plant. Mulching the plant helps the soil to stay moist. Do not fertilize until you see active growth.

Creating a new garden area for grasses.

Grasses in the Deep South

I called Pat McNeal, owner of a wholesale nursery that provides native and adapted plant species for landscaping purposes, from the smallest yards to the biggest of commercial and government construction projects. Pat also provides consulting and design work that focuses on finding plant solutions to very difficult engineering problems in the restoration of grasslands, woodlands, and natural and constructed watersheds. "What do you do," I asked, "about grasses down in Florida." "Well," he said, with a chuckle in his voice, "first thing to remember is that grasses in Florida can get big, very big. And if they are happy in the heat, a lot of grasses do exceptionally well. Like most places in the Southeast you have four basic conditions: light, shade, poor drainage, or good drainage.

"For full sun with soil ranging from well-drained to poorly drained there are some big grasses like sugar cane plume grass (*Erianthus giganteus*) and fakahatchee grass (*Tripsacum floradana* and *T. dactyloides*). Both are great specimen plants similar to Pampas grass for large spaces, the first with high-stemmed plumes and the second without plumes. The dwarf form of fakahatchee grass is especially fine for borders, mass plantings, and as a ground cover.

"And let's not forget the cord grasses (*Spartina* spp.) and, for poorly drained areas, especially in the shade, there are a wealth of sedges which have the added advantage of being mostly evergreen. For upland and well-drained sites in full sun there are a host of muhly grasses such as Gulf Coast muhly (*Muhlenbergia capillaris* and *M. filipes*). These are very nice clumping grasses that range in size from two feet to six feet across. There are also some very nice other native grasses like broomsedge bluestem (*Andropogon virginicus*), bushy bluestem (*A. glomeratus*), and the panic grasses (*Panicum* spp.).

Pampas grass is a stately specimen plant.

"For well-drained and shady areas there are great species like inland sea oats (*Chasmanthium latifolium*), pine winter grass (*Stipa avenacea*), and the wild ryes (*Elymus* spp.).

Pat also reminds the gardener that in Florida it's often not necessary to cut back the perennial grasses, fertilize, or water established grasses if you have planted the correct species for your soil type and climate. And according to McNeal it's important to know your soil. There are always the physical properties like drainage and moisture retention, plus chemical properties like nutritional content, including the amount of organic matter in your soil and pH, since Florida soils are often alkaline and many grasses prefer a more acidic soil.

"As to water," he said, "until root systems are fully developed, grasses need additional watering during dry periods. If you plant in the fall there is usually enough soil moisture to support good growth until the warm season begins in the spring."

Dividing Grasses

Clumping grasses, such as the species of *Miscanthus* and *Pennisetum*, grow out from the center, with the clumps getting larger every year. After a number of years the plants begin to die out in the center and will need dividing. Warm-season grasses are best divided in late winter and early spring. Cool-season grasses should be divided in fall or early spring.

Be warned: Dividing the big grasses is a major job requiring a good shovel, a landscaper's pole or crowbar for leverage, sharp shears, a small tree-pruning saw or electric hedge trimmer, and perhaps a good sharp ax. Cut the clumps in two or three sections, cut back the foliage by a third to compensate for loss of moisture and damaged roots, and replant.

Divide warm-season grasses like fountain grass in late winter or early spring.

Starting Grasses from Seed

Grasses grow beautifully from seed and sometimes that's the only way to acquire one of the newest cultivars. And if you don't mind the wait, seeds are much less expensive than buying plants, especially if you have a great deal of land to cover. When dealing with annuals, starting from seed is probably the best route.

If you have late spring frosts, as we often do here in the mountains around Asheville, it's best to start your seeds indoors, in a greenhouse or a heated cold frame. In areas of the Southeast with gentler climates, you can start seeds directly outdoors.

Melica altissima 'Atropurpurea' setting seed.

Store seeds in a cool, dry place until you need them. If storing them for a month or more, place the packets in a covered jar and keep them on a refrigerator shelf, but not the freezer.

When germinating seeds you will need a growing mix, containers to hold the mix, and—if you don't have a warm spot to keep temperatures above 65°F—a soil-heating cable or heated mat. Seeds resent cold, wet soil.

You'll find a wealth of containers at your garden center. These containers are usually made of pressed peat or pressed fibers and come in widths of three inches or two and one-fourth inches, round or square.

The growing mix should be lightweight and reasonably porous, and retain moisture. Various prepared mixes are available, usually formulated from peat moss and vermiculite or perlite. You can make your own, but it's time consuming and messy. Better to buy a commercial mix with all the work done for

you—and they are sterile, too. Damping-off, a fungal disease of seedlings, results from using nonsterile mixes.

Wet the mix by putting it in a plastic bag, slowly adding water, and kneading it. You want it moist, but not wet. Next, fill your containers, leaving about a fourth of an inch of space at the top. Now pat down the mix.

Seed packets will tell you how deep to plant the seeds and if light is needed for germination. If there are no directions, use these guidelines: Cover seeds a sixteenth of an inch or deeper, to the thickness of one seed. For tiny seeds like those of cloud grass (*Agrostis* spp.), don't cover them at all—just settle them on the surface of the mix with a light spray of water.

Cover the seed containers with plastic kitchen wrap or use a polyethylene bag to make a mini-greenhouse. Label each pot with the plant's name and the date.

When Shoots Appear

When the first green shoots appear, move the containers into a place with sunlight or under a special lighting fixture used for seed flats. Remove the plastic covers to let in fresh air. When the mix starts to dry out, carefully water the seedlings using room temperature water (cold water can shock the plants).

After the first grass leaves appear, begin using a diluted liquid fertilizer, especially if the growing mix did not contain nutrients. Then, as the seedlings grow, transplant them to larger containers. Thin them out, leaving one inch between each plant. Finally, move each seedling to its own pot.

Out in the Garden

When they are seedlings, most ornamental grasses look alike and often look like weeds. So it's important that you transplant seedlings to a well-prepared nursery bed that is clean of all weeds. Label each plant or row of plants.

When seedlings are one to two inches tall, thin them out to six to twelve inches apart. If moving them to containers, pot to larger sizes as the plants grow.

Summing It All Up

Here are around-the-seasons suggestions for ornamental grass care in the Southeast.

Spring: Remember to plant and transplant warm-season grasses when the weather settles. Remember to weed grasses and mulch, to conserve water and keep a check on weeds. Plant container-grown grasses and provide afternoon shade for new transplants.

Many grasses do well in pots.

Summer: Water grasses that are not drought tolerant when needed. Check every day for watering grasses in containers. Cut grasses for flower bouquets or drying when flowers or seedheads appear. Remove seedheads from weedy grasses such as *Pennisetum* 'Moudry'. Fluff up old mulch and add new mulch where needed. Plant cool-season grasses in late summer or early fall.

Fall: Plant cool-season grasses early in the fall. Collect and store seeds of grasses for next year. Pull and compost annual grasses. Cut back broken stems and damaged leaves. Divide crowded and overgrown clumping grasses.

Winter: Cut last year's grasses down to about six inches from the ground before new growth begins. Site and then plant new grasses. Order seeds and plants to get an early start on the season ahead. Start seeds indoors. Begin planting cool-season grasses when weather is mild.

A summer display of sedges and sedum.

THE ANNUAL GRASSES

The annual ornamental grasses are rarely grown for their foliage, which, in most cases, looks rather weedy. Except for a few variegated species, or the marvelously toned leaves of one corn cultivar, these annuals are best overlooked. But the flowers and the seeds of grasses number among the most beautiful plants in the annual category.

A few of the species listed in this chapter demand a place in the border or the garden bed proper because of their glorious flowers and seedheads. The rest are best grown in a cutting garden where they can be gathered at the proper stage of growth and either used for fresh cut flowers or dried for a stunning winter bouquet. Remember, too, that seed should be gathered for use in next year's garden, and properly stored in a cool, dry place until the following spring.

As a general rule, to promote adequate growth and full flowering, annual grasses require a garden spot in full summer sun. Most are not fussy about soil conditions because, regardless of their temporary home, they are programmed by their DNA to germinate, grow, blossom, and form seeds in one season.

Annual rice, *Oryza sativa*, in bloom.

You can start propagation of annual grasses in peat pots or other containers beginning a few weeks before your area's last expected frost, or you can plant seed directly outdoors—the timing depends on the hardiness of the grass species. I usually start some seeds indoors in early spring because a few types take days to germinate. When the first seed leaves emerge, give the seedlings plenty of light to prevent leggy growth.

Several terms you will see here refer to the hardiness of plants, and originated in England and Europe. "Hardy" annuals (HA) bear seed that can be planted directly outdoors at any time when the ground is workable, including late fall and very early spring; "half-hardy" annuals (HHA) can withstand only a little real cold; and the "tender" annuals (TA) cannot be planted outdoors until all frost dangers are past.

When planting annual grasses directly outdoors, prepare and mark the seedbed with care. The new little plants look for all the world like any other grassy weed, which can lead to confusion and dismay. A few seasons ago I was careless and a whole patch of hare's-tail grass was squeezed out by a local panic grass before I realized what was happening.

When seedlings are one to two inches tall, thin them out, allowing six to twelve inches between each plant, depending on their ultimate height. Be generous with seed, as the small grasses look much better when planted in substantial groupings of the same species.

Agrostis nebulosa

Agrostis nebulosa (HA), or cloud grass, is an aptly named ornamental annual that hails from Europe in general and Spain and the Iberian Peninsula in particular. The genus contains some one hundred species, some native to the United States, but none as lovely as this species.

The genus name is from the Greek word *agrostis*, derived from *agros* or "field," and refers to a kind of grass that grows in fields or open grasslands. The species name *nebulosa* means "cloudy," and once you see this grass in bloom you quickly realize it's aptly named.

This grass grows in tufts about eighteen inches tall. The culms have swollen nodes and bear scant foliage. The white to pinkish flowers bloom in summer, usually through July and August, and are followed by tiny seeds. They look much like miniature baby's breath (*Gypsophila* spp.). Although the plants are not long-lived, they are among the most attractive for bordering a garden walkway, tucked into the rock garden, or massed in the front of the border. And for all their delicate appearance, the seedheads are tough and resist shattering, so they can be picked for cut flowers or saved for winter bouquets. These panicles are often half as long as the plant. For the best cloud effect, prepare large clumps.

Plants do best in Zones 5 to 7. Sow seeds in spring or fall. They adapt to most soils but resent poor drainage. While cloud grass does its best in full sun, it will accept light shade.

Plants can become a pest through reseeding, so remove the seedheads before they mature. They can also be grown in pots and will do well indoors if provided with plenty of light.

Avena sterilis (HA), or animated oats, is a short-lived annual with a prominent awn. Awns are spike-like or bristle-like projections or appendages that stick out from spikelets, and in this species can be almost three inches long. *Avena* is an old Latin name for oats; *sterilis* refers to the fact that the basal spikelet, the vegetative plant, and embryo in the ripe seed represent three successive generations, yet

Avena fatua and *Avena sterilis*

remain together as the seedling grows. This grass originated around the Mediterranean and central Asia.

The grass in bloom is very attractive and is a good addition to the middle of the border. When cut green, the panicles can be used with other cut flowers, or in winter bouquets when dried.

Animated oats has another reason for long popularity: Those long awns, when placed on a moist blotter or other damp surface, will twist and turn as they absorb and then evaporate moisture.

Long ago in Norse mythology, animated oats was known as Loki's grass or dwarf's grass, and people believed that Loki used the twisting of the grass as messages of evil to mortals. That awn was also called the leg of an Arabian spider and used in telling fortunes. Tellers would place awns in front of them, wet them with a drop of water, then call out various threats and predictions as the awns twisted and writhed. In Scotland, these oat awns were used as bait on salmon hooks.

Animated oats will adapt to most soil types, likes full sun, and will reseed with a vengeance, so

the plants are best cut to the ground before seeds mature. Best in Zones 6 to 8.

Avena fatua (HA), or wild oats, is considered—at least by farmers—to be a weed. But the plants, while scraggly at best, have very attractive flower panicles in a beautiful shade of light brown. The species name is from the Latin word *fatuous*, meaning "taste-less," as the plant has no food value.

Briza maxima (HHA), or quaking grass, is a native of southern Europe and has been in cultivation as a garden ornamental for well over two hundred years. The genus name, *Briza*, is Greek for "sleepy" or "nodding," referring to the dangling spikelets waving in the wind. The species term *maxima* means it's the largest grass in the genus.

The spikelets quiver and quake with every gentle movement of a summer breeze, looking a lot like Quaker Puffed Wheat, the popular cereal that was "shot from guns" and often found on the breakfast table when I was young. In addition, the lemmas (the parts that enclose the flowers) are faintly striped with purple, making these very attractive flowering plants. The grasses grow about three feet tall and the seedheads are about an inch long, suspended on threadlike stems. Because of these wiry attachments, the individual spikelets twist and turn in the slightest breeze. They are beautiful in the middle of the border, bunched, or collected for winter bouquets. Unlike many grasses, the flowering panicles are quite tough and hold together for a long time in the garden, so you can cut them throughout the season.

Provide full sun and a well-drained soil. Quaking grasses are best sowed directly in the

Briza minor and *Briza maxima*

garden when significant frost danger has past. These grasses are most effective when planted in large clumps.

For dried flowers, gather the spikelets as they begin to turn brown but before they begin to shatter. Hang them upside down in loose bunches.

Briza minor (HHA) is little quaking grass, and if the epithet "cute" can be correctly applied to a grass, it fits this species. The flower clusters are miniature versions of quaking grass, *Briza maxima*.

Bromus brizaeformis (HA), also known as rattlesnake brome or rattlesnake chess, is the most beautiful of this genus. The genus name is taken from the ancient Greek word *bromas*, meaning "oat," from the word *broma* or "food." The species *brizaeformis* refers to the similarity of the seedheads to those of the quaking grasses (*Briza*).

As a genus the bromes are weedy grasses mostly introduced from Europe. At one time credulous farmers were convinced that with certain changes in the weather, wheat would turn into chess or cheat grass. Others thought that if many of the bromes were mixed with wheat the result could be a hallucinogenic treat. To my knowledge, neither is true.

Rattlesnake brome is an upright annual or sometimes biennial that has an open and airy growth habit. The plants are about two feet high upon maturity, with flat leaf blades of a medium green color. The flowering and fruiting occurs from June to July.

If flowers are cut before they ripen, the blooming stems make very decorative additions to both fresh and dried arrangements. Seed this grass in clumps and grow them where the attractive spikelets move in every little summer breeze, surrounded by perennials.

Provide a good, well-drained garden soil, in full sun, and seed directly in the garden.

Bromus brizaeformis

Coix lacryma-jobi (HHA), or Job's tears, sometimes known as Christ's tears, is a close relative of corn and has the distinction of being one of the oldest ornamental grasses in cultivation. It was probably being grown for pleasure (as opposed to being grown as a crop) in the fourteenth century, especially around religious institutions. When planting this grass in your backyard, you have history just outside the door. The genus *Coix* is a Greek word for a palm or reed-leaved plant, while *lacryma-jobi* literally means "Job's tears."

In *The Graminae*, Agnes Arber writes about a Chinese general who conquered Tongking in the first century of the Christian era and became so fond of the Job's tears that he carried several cartloads of seeds back home. An annual grass (a short-lived perennial in very warm climates, this grass grows beautifully in Zone 10), Job's tears is native to Southeast Asia and is also found in grasslands at the foothills of the Himalayas.

Culms are knobby, often bending at the nodes, and bear glossy, deep green leaf blades, up to two feet long and sometimes two inches wide, graced with wavy edges. In very warm surroundings, plants can reach a height of five to six feet.

The flowering and fruiting terminal spikelets are nondescript but eventually mature into shiny,

pea-sized receptacles that hold very hard, beadlike, gray or mottled seeds resembling teardrops. The seeds bear two feathery female stigmas just below two green male flowers.

Considered a weed by many farmers, the seeds are also a valuable foodstuff which, after being pounded and threshed, can be mixed with water to make an edible cereal used as a nutritious drink, much like barley water. Old travel books describe locals husking the seeds and eating them like peanuts. Fermented drinks are also made from these grains. Throughout the tropics, the seeds are often colored, then strung and sold as rosaries. Certain Burmese tribes use the seeds in combination with squirrels' tails, beetles' wings, and hammered silver as jewelry. But Arber also notes that "under cultivation the shells soon lose their hard, pearly quality and rich gloss, and become relatively soft."

The plants will easily adapt to wet ground, so they do well growing next to ponds or streams. They also tolerate soils that lack fertility, but do not respond to heavy clay soils. Remember to soak the seeds for twenty-four hours before planting. They grow well in Zones 8 through 12; in colder areas start the seeds indoors in individual peat pots.

Rarely, a variegated variety is sold under the name of 'Aurea Zebrina' with leaves striped longitudinally with green and white.

Coix lacryma-jobi

Eleusine coracana (HHA), known in the horticultural trade as goose grass or 'Green Cat', is known to most of the world as African millet. "Goose" refers to the look of the blooming spikes. Other common names include ragi, coracan millet, and finger millet, the last because the seed-topped stems look like cartoon fingers. This grass is named for Eleusis, a Greek town about ten miles west of Athens, where Demeter was worshiped.

The species name *coracana* refers to *coracan*, the Indian name for this grain.

This species is a cultivated form of *Eleusine indica*, a plant grown for food among the people of Africa and southern Asia. The seeds provide a valuable food, and a fermented beer is made from the grain. In the mid-1990s, the annual global production of this grass was about twenty-eight million tons, with some twenty-two million tons for human needs. The seedheads also make great cut flowers and are easily dried for winter bouquets.

The culms stand erect, have a fibrous root system, and grow about two feet tall, with the two- to three-inch spikelets usually curved in at the tip, much like the claws on a cat. When in bloom the leaves are hardly seen. This species also does very well in poor soil, but likes full sun and good drainage.

Eleusine coracana

In late February start seeds indoors and keep them warm. After germination provide plenty of light. When large enough to handle, transplant seedlings to individual pots or trays, and never plant outdoors until all danger of frost is past.

⸱—⸱—⸱—⸱—⸱—⸱—⸱—⸱—⸱—⸱—⸱—⸱—⸱—⸱—⸱—

Eragrostis tef (TA), the love grass, was once called *Eragrostis abyssinica*, and the ancient

Eragrostis tef

Ethiopian name for this plant is *teff*. Long grown in India and Australia as a forage plant, it's also found in Africa, where the seeds are ground for flour and used in making bread. Teff is also used for brewing alcoholic drinks, and teff straw is used to reinforce mud or plaster used in building construction. Except for a few species that provide forage on grazing lands of the Southwest and a few others used for erosion control, the numerous American species have little agricultural value. The generic name is from the Greek *eros*, or "love," and *agrostis*, a kind of grass.

When in bloom, teff is such an attractive grass that it belongs in every border. More than three feet high, the plants spread out, especially when loaded with seeds. Not only are plants attractive in bloom, as autumn approaches the leaves turn a beautiful light tan and persist until storms bend the plants to the ground.

Teff does very well when planted in a good, humus-rich soil, in a sunny spot. In warmer climates, plants will usually bloom from seed in four months of growth. If you want early bloomers, start by germinating seeds in a greenhouse. Sow the seeds on a good growing mix, and move seedlings to individual pots as soon as they are large enough to handle.

~~~~~~~~~~~~~~~~~~~~~~~~~~~~~~~~~~

Hordeum jubatum (HA) has the common names of fox-tail barley or squirrel's-tail grass. You will often see it blooming along the roadsides and at the edges of interstates, where the flowers glisten in the afternoon sunlight. *Hordeum* is the old Latin name for barley, and the species name of *jubatum* (from the Latin *juba* for an ancient King of Numidea) refers to the mane-like appearance of the silvery awns.

Hordeum jubatum

Plants grow about a foot high and in midsummer produce dense nodding spikes of pale green or silvery-purple tints, up to four inches long. Be forewarned, as they are very weedy.

Provide any good garden soil with a place in full sun and remember to pick blossoms well before they ripen, as these spikelets shatter easily.

~~~~~~~~~~~~~~~~~~~~~~~~~~~~~~~~~~

Lagurus ovatus

Lagurus ovatus (HA), or hare's-tail grass, is the only species in the genus, a short-lived annual plant originally from the Mediterranean region and southern Europe. Sometimes called rabbit-tail grass, the generic name is from the Greek *lagos*, for "hare" and *oura* for "tail," referring to the woolly seedheads. *Ovatus* describes the oval or egg-shape of the bloom.

The foliage is a light green and the stems and leaves are soft with a fine down. Besides being attractive, the flower heads do not shatter with age. The seedheads are widely mistreated by people who feel the necessity to continually "improve" on nature and dye these little bunnies electric pink, green, or yellow, then sell them in cheap plastic vases to weary drivers at interstate and throughway rest-stops.

Although the plants are short-lived, you can have a long season by staggering their propagation. Sow seeds in trays or pots using good seed compost and keeping the seeds in a warm place until they germinate. Sow seeds in March to April. Transplant seedlings when they are large enough to handle. Seed can also be sown outdoors in mid-spring. Provide a good, well-drained soil in full sun.

Use these grasses bunched in the border, along garden pathways, in rock gardens, or in pots, where they grow beautifully.

Lagurus ovatus 'Nanus' is a dwarf cultivar with plants rarely exceeding six inches in height. The only way to describe this grass is incredibly cute.

Lamarkia aurea (TA), or golden top (sometimes it's called toothbrush grass), is another one-species genus, this one named in honor of J. B. Lamarck, the French naturalist whose theories on evolution were scoffed at by his contemporaries though they greatly influenced Darwin. *Aurea* refers to the golden yellow color of the blooms. Golden top is one beautiful grass and, if it were a perennial, every knowledgeable gardener in the world would grow it. The one-sided panicles have a shimmering golden effect when fresh that becomes silvery with age. By midsummer the plants are already turning brown, so stagger seed sowings to have flowers until fall. Seed was introduced from the Mediterranean region into the far western states.

Lamarkia aurea

Plants can reach an eighteen-inch height but usually check in at about a foot. The plants have a tendency to spread.

Provide full sun and a well-drained but moist soil.

Oryza sativa, or rice, is cultivated in all the warm countries where there's sufficient water to support its growth. One of the food staples of the world, feeding billions of people, it's also a decorative annual grass in its own right. The genus name is from *oruza*, the old Greek name for rice, and *sativa* is the Latin word for "sow," or "planting by seed."

Oryza sativa

The grass is a loosely tufted annual, generally reaching six feet high with stout stems, leaf blades up to five feet long, and a loosely branched panicle that turns one-sided with age. It's a wetland plant so must have its feet in water and, even in Zone 7, you will need to start the seeds indoors with bottom heat. After the seedlings are between three and six inches high, you can transplant them either into a marsh or shallow water in the water garden. They cannot go outside until all danger of frost or chill is past. Regular rice is usually grown for the decorative value of the dried panicles.

A variety known as 'Nigrescens', thought to have first evolved in Japan, bears leaves of a rich, dark purple. The beautiful foliage makes it a valuable addition to the water garden.

◡◠◡◠◡◠◡◠◡◠◡◠◡◠◡◠◡◠◡◠◡◠◡◠◡

Panicum capillare, known as old witch grass, is a species detested by farmers but really quite attractive in the garden. It has large brittle flower heads that, like tumbleweeds, easily break away from the main stem and blow about in the wind. Because of this, I hesitate to recommend it but if found in your garden, give it some small place to lend its charm.

Panicum miliaceum

Panicum capillare

Panicum miliaceum, broomcorn millet, is also known as hog millet, Indian millet, and proso. *Panicum* is a large genus of useful grasses, from an old Latin word, *panicum*, which refers to the common millet or *Setaria italica*. Grown as a food crop for years, especially in India, China, and Japan, it's a very attractive ornamental grass for the garden border. The straw is used to make brooms, particularly folk art reproductions.

It's a loosely tufted annual that bears profusely branched panicles and lots of seeds. Height is usually around three feet with

flowering and fruiting in late summer. The seeds are a reddish brown and very attractive. A horticultural form with purple inflorescences is known as 'Violaceum'.

Provide full sun on a good fertile soil; plants are fairly drought tolerant.

This plant can be weedy so use a bit of care at the end of the season when the seeds could spread around the garden.

◡◠◡◠◡◠◡◠◡◠◡◠◡◠◡◠◡◠◡◠◡◠◡◠◡

Pennisetum glaucum 'Purple Majesty' (HHA), black millet, was the All-America Selections winner for the 2003 garden season and one of the most popular plants seeded in the trial gardens of the previous year. This glorious ornamental grass is a hybrid of pearl millet, or the foot grain (*Pennisetum glaucum*), also sometimes called the cattail or bulrush millet, and was developed at the University of Nebraska Institute of Agriculture by David Andrews and John Rajewski. *Pennisetum* refers to the Latin *penna*, or "feather," and *seta* or "bristle" alluding to the featherlike bristles of some species.

'Purple Majesty' has showy purple leaves with a red midrib and looks like a purple cornstalk topped with foot-long purple plumes covered with

Phalaris canariensis

Pennisetum glaucum 'Purple Majesty'

a pollen dusting. At maturity, plants are about five feet tall and two to three feet in diameter. In summer heat the plants are fast growing; they are drought tolerant but appreciate an evenly moist soil. Birds love the seeds.

Provide a well-drained and sunny site, as these grasses originally came from the tropics and like warm weather. Sunlight is important to intensify the purple color.

Phalaris canariensis (HA), or canary grass, is a native of the Canary Islands and southern Europe. Belonging to a large group of seed grasses, this species is used in most birdseed, especially for wild and domestic canaries. The other grains in most mixes are millet, linseed, and many cereal grains.

Canada exports the most canary grass—followed by Argentina and the United States—with shipments numbering in the tons. Because birdcage liners are often taken to landfills, canary grass is often seen growing at various town dumps.

The height ranges between three and four feet—and I hasten to add that the foliage of this grass is not especially attractive. But the seedheads are quite beautiful, consisting of spike-like panicles topped with terminal inflorescences bearing white spikelets, each with three prominent green stripes.

Seedheads will easily shatter, so pick them before they ripen, but even where seeds have fallen away, the empty spikelets are still attractive in dried bouquets.

Take a cue on growing conditions from the fact that plants do so well in landfills. Provide full sun and moist soil. Canary grass can naturalize in the Southeast and become an invasive weed.

Phalaris minor is known as small canary grass. It has attractive flower heads and is also used for birdseed. It rarely exceeds two feet in height.

Polypogon monspeliensis (HA), or rabbit's foot grass, sometimes called annual beard grass, is an attractive annual that brings a great look to any garden. Introduced to the United States from Europe, this plant was originally imported from Africa and parts of Asia. *Polypogon* is from the Greek *polus*, for "much," and *pogon*, for "beard," alluding to the bristly inflorescence. *Monspeliensis* refers to Montpellier in the south of France.

It's a loosely growing grass with several leaves, frequently branched at the base, with tufted stems about two feet tall, often bending at the nodes. From late spring on, they bear very dense, spike-like panicles up to six inches long, densely covered in fine bristles and usually a light green that slowly turns to light brown.

Polypogon monspeliensis

This grass succeeds in any good and well-drained garden soil in a sunny spot and, surprisingly, plants will also do well in moist ditches and along pool margins.

Setaria italica

Setaria italica (HA), or foxtail millet, is a striking annual grass that bears large, full panicles, often up to a foot long, that look exactly like a foxtail that might have been at home on the rumble seat of an old 1930s Chevy. Other common names include Italian millet, Japanese millet, Hungarian grass, Bengal grass, and *millet des oiseaux*. First cultivated in Ancient China around 2700 B.C., foxtail reached Europe during the Middle Ages, and entered the United States in 1849 as a fodder crop.

While the average plant height is a little over three feet, the panicles are often so large they bow to the ground with the weight of the many seeds. These grasses provide a great source of feed for wildlife, and if they bloom in your garden, you'll note a marked increase in the birds in your backyard. Cut the panicles before they ripen and add to fresh bouquets or allow them to mature and use them for dried bouquets.

Plants do best in good, well-drained garden soil in full sun. While they tolerate some lack of water, they do not take kindly to drought conditions.

Setaria lutescens, or foxtail grass, was originally a common weed in Europe, and has become a common weed in America. The

Triticum aestivum

bristles of the two-inch long panicles have a definite yellow-orange color that remains after the seedheads dry, and is very attractive in decorative arrangements. Use this grass in dense plantings for the seedheads to really stand up and out. Or grow it in a cutting garden, in both cases providing average soil and full sun.

Setaria viridis, or green foxtail grass, bears greenish spikelets and is often seen as a roadside weed. It's attractive in the cutting garden but too rangy for the formal border.

Sorghum bicolor var. technicus (HHA), or black sorghum, has been in continuous cultivation since prehistoric times. Over those millennia the seeds have been used to make flour and produce molasses, the dried panicles are used to make brooms, and a few species provide great silage and fodder for cattle. The genus name is from *sorgho*, the Italian name of the plant, with

Sorghum bicolor var. *technicus*

bicolor referring to the leaves, a light green color lightly spattered with brown, as though the pigment was applied by running your thumb across a toothbrush loaded with paint.

Sorghums are strong-growing plants with straight stems up to six feet tall, and often taller in warmer parts of the world. The leaf blades are broad, like corn, green at first then turning brown. They are about four inches wide and often up to three feet long, and tightly grasp the stems.

The flowers grow in a loose panicle up to a foot long, with many seeds that range in color from dark green to a deep brown and almost black.

Provide a good soil and full sun, remembering never to set this plant out in the garden until all danger of frost is past.

Triticum aestivum (HA) is wheat. Wheat is mainly used for flour, but it's also the source of alcoholic beverages, hay, the straw used for mats and carpets, and a starch for pastes and sizing for textiles.

No one really knows where the wheat plant as we know it today originated. L. W. Briggle, in *Introduction to Energy Use in Wheat Production,* wrote, "Wheat evolved from wild grasses, probably somewhere in the Near East. A very likely place of origin is the area known in early historical times as the Fertile Crescent—a region with rich soils in the upper reaches of the Tigris-Euphrates drainage basin."

Bearded wheat is a short-lived annual grass growing to about three feet, with medium to dark green leaves, straight stems, and a seedhead that is an erect, dense spike with many awns. Beardless wheat (a form of the same species) looks exactly like its relative but lacks the long awns.

Wheat belongs in the cutting garden where you can gather the flowering spikes for all sorts of decorative uses (many florists dye them improbable colors, often fuchsia and yellow). But kept to their natural color, wheat makes a splendid addition to any bouquet.

Plant the seeds in early spring and they will germinate in five to ten days. Provide a good garden soil in full sun.

Zea mays 'Quadricolor'

Zea mays var. gracillima 'Variegata'

(TA) is one of the decorative forms of corn, the only grain the Americas contributed to the world. Corn is a robust annual that needs lots of sunlight and warmth to survive; in northern Scotland, for example, it only grows in a greenhouse. The height can reach eight feet, or, as the song from *Oklahoma!* says, as high as "an elephant's eye!" The leaf sheaths tightly grasp the very thick stems, and the leaves themselves are two or more feet long. *Zea* is the old Greek word for a type of grain and *mays* is the Latin word for "maize," one of the time-honored names of corn.

The garden use of corn is limited to the variegated forms, of which *Zea mays* var. *gracillima* 'Variegata' is the smallest, with leaves striped a pure white and growing about two feet tall. *Zea mays* var. *japonica* reaches a height of four feet and bears leaves striped with white. *Zea mays* 'Quadricolor' is a slightly larger plant with leaves of white, yellow, and pink stripes on a green background.

Corn is a heavy feeder, so always plant the seeds in fertile soil and add more fertilizer monthly; it also likes plenty of water. Because corn is so sensitive to cold and takes time for development, start plants indoors in individual peat pots, transplanting as they grow. Try growing variegated corn in eight-inch pots, and group a few for an effective outdoor-terrace decoration.

For those gardeners with a delight in the strange, try the following cultivars for their colored ears.

Zea mays 'Indian Corn' produces six-foot plants with coarse green foliage, but by midsummer brings forth ears of corn with kernels in various shades of white, red, yellow, with some bicolored.

Zea mays 'Strawberry Corn' has medium green foliage with two- to six-inch

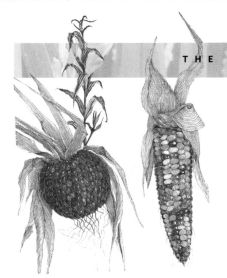

Zea mays 'Strawberry Corn' and 'Indian Corn'

rounded ears of corn of a rich reddish mahogany color, each packaged in straw-colored husks.

Zea mays var. **praecox**, or popcorn, has plants about five feet high bearing small ears of corn about six inches wide, variable in shape, and having small kernels, usually of a reddish mahogany, that can be popped.

Zizania aquatica (HA) is the wild rice of gourmet food stores, smart restaurants, and food co-ops, and a major source of food for Native Americans long before immigrants entered the country. Wild rice is also an important food for wildlife and is often planted at the edges of ponds, wetlands, or marshes for just that purpose. The Chinese cultivate the Asiatic species (*Z. latifolia*), calling it *kau sun*.

Zizanion is an old Greek name for a weed found growing in grain fields (this weed was described in the Bible and known as tares). *Aquatica* refers to water.

Wild rice can reach a height of eight feet. The stems bear flat blades and large terminal panicles, with the lower branches spreading down and bearing the female flowers and eventually grains of rice. The upper branches grow upward and bear the male flowers, which eventually fall off.

Wild rice is especially attractive in a waterside setting. Even a small pool can boast a few plants, especially if the grass is planted in clay pots, later to be submerged. Put the grasses in clay pots with well-fertilized soil, covering the soil with gravel (to prevent fouling the water with dirt), and submerge the pots at the pool's edge.

Obviously the following method of harvest would not be possible in a suburban pond, but in *Edible Wild Plants*, Oliver Perry Medsger described how Native American women collected wild rice in a canoe. The first woman slowly paddled the canoe along the rice beds, while the second held a stick in each hand and, bending the stalks over the edge of the boat with one stick, struck the stalks with the other, knocking the grain into the bottom of the canoe. Then they took the grains and either dried them in the sun or threshed them by stamping them under their feet.

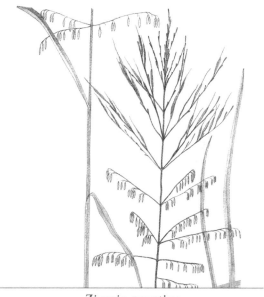

Zizania aquatica

THE PERENNIAL GRASSES

Back in the early 1970s I ordered a selection of perennial grasses from an English nursery. There were many forms to fill out and dates to be circled on the calendar because, even then, import restrictions were rife because of possible exotic invasive plants. Days passed and finally the package arrived, stamped and re-stamped and sealed and resealed, the predominate labels being a particular pier in New York City.

Grabbing my utility knife, I cut through the tape and opened the box to find that all the grasses were stone dead, apparently having evaporated their collective water days ago. But wait! There was a slight movement in the parched roots. Under my watchful eye, a lone English ant stumbled out of the plastic and wandered over the backyard grass to meet its American cousins.

That was my last attempt to import plants in the time-honored way. Now my new grass adventures revolve around more local nursery supplies and growing new plants from seed, which are probably more reliable approaches in the long run.

Giant reed grass, maiden grass, fountain grass, and blue fescue.

Perennial grasses are valuable elements in both the garden proper and in pots on your deck. The following grasses are perennials from a wide range of countries around the world. These are stalwart additions to any garden, their beauty apparent in the leafy silhouettes, the striking flowers and seedheads, the various shapes and textures of the blades, the colors, and, finally, their ease of care.

Perennial Grasses in the South

It's one thing to write about growing a wide range of ornamental grasses in areas where the climate fights your efforts only for a few months during the year. It's quite another where the weather, sunny at the beach and impossibly hot everywhere else, including areas that were never fully settled until the widespread use of the air conditioner. So among the following grasses are many that can take the heat, many that love the sun, and a lot more that will do well only in specialized conditions. Several are so beautiful that if your garden is too cold to accommodate them year-round, I've suggested growing them in pots and bringing them indoors for the winter. And I have included some cool-season grasses that do resent the heat and humidity found in much of the South because they often perform beautifully if you garden in areas with some elevation (such as my garden in Asheville). In these areas they often are very attractive until Old Sol waxes to full scorching glory in the summer. As John Greenlee often points out, "If you can't grow a number of grasses in a hot Southern summer, how about brightening your winter garden, using cool-weather perennial grasses as annuals?" *Festuca ovina* 'Golden Toupee' might rebel against the heat and humidity of summer in southern Florida, but it makes a great winter annual.

Festuca glauca 'Golden Toupee'

A garden including a variety of perennial grasses.

I have tried to include most of the grasses available today on the market (and I know I've forgotten or overlooked a few and, if so, let me know). But remember, nurseries are motivated by profit, just like other businesses. So don't expect the majority of the so-called "box stores" to feature an elegant *Stipa* in their perennial collection (although surprises still happen). But good nursery and garden centers will often honor a request or two from loyal customers, and probably would stock *Miscanthus* 'Cabaret' if they thought anybody wanted it.

Then, too, with today's usually fast trucking and the mail-order nurseries' knowledge of packing, there's no reason not to buy by mail or from the Internet. And don't forget seeds. An astounding number of grasses are available by seed, so if trapped high on a mountain somewhere in north Georgia, with only the post office down the road, you can still have an elegant garden just by growing plants from seed.

Stipa tenuissima

Alopecurus pratensis var. aureus, or yellow foxtail grass, is a beauty. The generic name is from the Greek *alopex*, "fox," and *oura*, "tail," referring to the cylindrical panicles of flowers, and the specific name means that the plant grows in meadows. It's an upright, mostly clumping perennial that slowly spreads with creeping rhizomes. Height is up to two feet. The blades are a fourth of an inch wide and a bright golden yellow with a green midrib. Unfortunately, the common name infers a more prominent bloom than nature provides, so this grass is grown entirely for the colorful blades. For some years I grew it at the edge of a wall in our lakeside garden where plants received eight hours of sunlight, but the grasses were shaded from hot noon sun by the airy

Alopecurus pratensis var. *aureus* (foreground)

branches of a big, white Meidiland rose. There, foxtail joined forces with some oriental poppies and bulbous oat grass, another plant that dislikes summer heat. In an average hot and dry Asheville, this grass would recede for a rest until cooler weather arrived in mid-September. Then it was again a star until hit by frost. Provide a good, moist, well-drained soil. Zones 6 to 9.

Ammophila breviligulata, or American beach grass, is known by every beach-walker from the dunes of Fire Island to the blowing sands of the North and South Carolina shores. It's a rhizomatous, sod-forming perennial that is a Godsend to beaches under the threat of erosion from either wave or wind. The waving blades grow about forty inches tall and in late summer produce sandy-yellow cylindrical flower clusters

Ammophila breviligulata

borne on tall stems. The scientific name is derived from the Greek *ammos*, for "sand," and *philos*, for "loving," and that's exactly what this grass delights in (the species refers to an anatomical detail of no interest to gardeners). While not overly attractive, especially when compared to many of the grasses in this book, it has such stellar value that I include it here. A cultivar called 'Hatteras' (for the cape of the same name) is best for Southern beaches. Propagation is by seed or division, but plant in early spring or wait for fall so they have a chance to acclimate before the sand heats up in summer. Zones 6 to 10.

Andropogon gerardii, big bluestem or turkey-foot grass, is one of America's great native prairie grasses, its robust growth and six-foot height (occasionally up to nine feet) making it a great foil for a bright blue summer sky. At one time big bluestem was the most important constituent of the wild hay of the prairie states. But continual development and poor land management have taken their toll. The blades turn a beautiful shade of light reddish-brown after the approach of frost but persist throughout the winter. The plants prefer water and are not as luxuriant when grown on poor and dry soil, but once rooted, they will survive. The scientific name is derived from the Greek *aner* or "man" and *pogon* for "beard," referring to the white stalks of the individual spikelets. The inflorescence consists of three (or multiples of three) stalks that resemble a turkey's foot.

This grass is a warm-season species and has great virtue as a natural hedge of grass or planted along the edge of a woodland, or massed in the wild garden (it and its seeds are important foods for birds and other animals). It's native to all the states of the Southeast, and can be found growing from the east until it comes up short at Nevada and California.

Patience is needed if you raise plants from seed because very little happens above ground for the first year; most of the plant's energy is spent sending down roots that eventually reach a ten-

Andropogon gerardii

foot depth. With such extensive root systems, the grasses have protection from excessive droughts and prairie fires, which allow it to thrive in hot, dry sites under full sun. Zones 4 to 10.

Andropogon glomeratus, the bushy bluestem, is a smaller species usually reaching four feet, with flowering spikelets clustered at the tops of the stems. This grass is at its best when near a waterside, along streams, and in bogs, not to mention in tubs where ample water is guaranteed. Obviously, it prefers a damper soil than big bluestem. Zones 5 to 10.

Andropogon glomeratus

Andropogon ternarius, the split beard bluestem, is a true native of the Southeast, being at home on the Atlantic coastal plain, then south to Florida and west to Texas and Oklahoma. This very attractive grass prefers a dry, well-drained site and is great for controlling erosion on steep slopes.

The leaves grow in clumps usually more than a foot tall and as wide, while the flower spikes can soar to a five-foot height. The cottony racemes appear in pairs and are very attractive in bloom and when cut for floral arrangements. Zones 6 to 9.

Andropogon virginicus

Andropogon virginicus, the broom sedge, is at home across much of America (except New England), from the East Coast, west to Texas and Oklahoma. It prefers moist sandy soil and is quite at home in low pine barrens. These grasses perform best in partial sun or shade on soils best described as rather "used." While not in its prime in the perennial border, this grass shines at providing an efficient and attractive ground cover and, like little bluestem, is great to see waving in a winter's wind. Propagate by seed or division in the spring. Zones 5 to 9.

Anemanthele lessoniana, or New Zealand wind grass, is new to the trade, this being the first year that a major seed nursery has offered seed. I saw it two summers ago at the Edinburgh Botanic Garden, where the clumping, then arching, stems of this strangely beautiful grass were amply adorned with purple-tinged flower heads that

Anemanthele lessoniana

good, moist, well-drained garden soil with added organic matter. Zones 8 to 9.

Anthoxanthum odoratum, or sweet vernal grass, is not grown for ornament, but when it comes to gardening, it never hurts to end a busy day with something cool and refreshing. Sweet vernal grass can be used to add the fragrance of the meadow to your favorite spirit or wine. This grass contains the chemical coumarin, which imparts a sweet aromatic principle to the plants. By adding three or four blades of this grass to a quart of spirits, in a week or so the sweet odor is imparted to the alcohol in the bottle. The plants reach a height of eighteen inches and are found growing wild throughout the Southeast, except for Florida. The generic name is taken from the Greek *anthos*, "flower," and *xanthos*, "yellow," referring to the yellow inflorescence. Zones 5 to 9.

brightened the feathery culms. While evergreen in warmer climates, the dark green leaves can, under stress, be streaked with pale brown touches of color. Clumps are about four feet tall. The blossoms appear in midsummer on delicate stems.

Today, it's best acquired by starting your own seedlings. Just pay attention to a few suggestions: Use a sterile seed mix; use a heating cable to provide continuous 70° F temperatures; and cover the seeds with just a fine sprinkling of sterile sand or vermiculite to avoid excluding daytime illumination, because light helps in the germination, which can take up to three months.

Wind grass is tolerant of full sun, but in the Deep South should be provided with light shade in the heat of the midday sun. Provide a

Aristida purpurea, purple three-awn grass or purple needle grass, is another native found growing in dry hills and plains from Texas to southern California. These densely tufted, upright grasses are named for the Latin *arista*, or "awn," referring to the conspicuous awns found in this genus. With its large and twisted inflorescence, with its awns seeming to go in all directions, this grass is great for naturalizing in a meadow, along the woodland edge, or in front of a large stone in a hilly rock garden. But, be warned, the needle-like awns easily stick to clothing and dogs, cats being too close to the ground to usually come in contact with them. Flowers are perfect for flower arrangements. Zones 6 to 9.

Arrhenatherum elatius var. *bulbosum* **'Variegatum'**, or bulbous oats grass, is a cool-season perennial with a mouthful of a scientific name. The genus is a combination of the Greek word *arren* for "male" and *anther* for "awn," referring to the bristled male flowers. *Bulbosum* pertains to the bulblets that are storage organs, especially for water, at the base of the stems, and 'Variegatum' to the white longitudinal stripes on the deep green blades. Each of the little bulblets will produce another plant. Plants are usually about a foot high.

Because it's a cool-season grass, it performs best in spring and in the fall after the heat of midsummer is over. In the South it prefers partial shade and seems to adjust to a sweeter

Arrhenatherum elatius var. *bulbosum* 'Variegatum'

soil; in my garden they are planted at the edge of a shady wall. In milder winters they are usually evergreen. Unlike many grasses, both the cultivar and the rarer species will adapt to pots and survive indoors if given enough light. Provide a good, moist but well-drained soil with added humus. On occasion, especially in damp summers, these grasses will contract a leaf fungus in the class *Hyphomycete*. Zones 5 to 9.

Arundo donax, or the giant reed grass, originally came from the Mediterranean region and was probably first introduced into America when it arrived in California around the early 1800s.

Several products are derived from this grass. Reeds for clarinets, bassoons, and oboes are all crafted from cut pieces of its culms, as the pipes for primitive pipe organs once were. Like bamboo, giant reed stems are also used as fishing rods, and their cut sections are used in basket making.

In California this grass is called wild cane. In the wild it can reach thirty feet high, with a tough root system that reaches deeply into the soil. The blue-green leaves are up to two inches wide and a foot long, with flowers appearing in late summer, in dense plume-like panicles often two feet long.

In addition to aesthetic purposes, giant reed grasses were once used as windbreaks—as was *Spartina*, another native grass—and as thatching for sod houses. But when used to control erosion, it sometimes becomes invasive.

Giant reed can grow into dense hummocks of gigantic culms that offer nothing to wildlife, except holding mud in place. When dried, the culms can become major fire hazards. Their speedy growth crowds out native plants, so be careful where you locate this beauty.

Unlike most other grasses, giant reed can be propagated from stem cuttings. Take a mature stem from your fall garden, remove all the foliage, then take a plastic tray, and fill it with about two inches of water. Cut the grass cane to fit the pan and float it on the water's surface, keeping the water warm. Within a few weeks, shoots will appear at the leaf axils, then roots will appear below the shoots. By late winter the plants will be ready to move into damp, almost wet, compost; then slowly let the compost dry. Plant roots formed to absorb oxygen directly from water must be acclimated to solid soil before they're able to do their job. Zones 7 to 10.

Arundo donax 'Variegata'

Arundo donax

Arundo donax 'Variegata' is similar to the species, but the leaves have stripes of green and a creamy yellow-white. The stripes are at their best in spring and, with the heat of summer, the yellow

tints usually disappear. Of the two, this is the better one to put in the garden because the variegations mean the leaves have less chlorophyll, thus produce less food, so the aggressive habits of the giant reed are considerably reduced. In my garden this grass sits in front of and fights it out with a large clump of zebra grass, just behind a beautiful native *Hibiscus coccineus*, a combination that has now persisted for five years. This grass usually stays between six and twelve feet in height. Zones 6 to 10.

Arundo pliniana, or Plinio's reed grass, comes from Eurasia and grows wild along parts of the Italian coast. The leaves have a blue cast, and are about an inch wide and three to five inches long, growing in clumps up to ten feet tall. The leaves are very sharp edged and can easily cut an unwary hand. The very attractive blooms open in fluffy panicles. Not very common, it is now a collector's choice and is especially attractive in pots or tubs. There is the potential for this to be an invasive grass. This grass needs a moist, fertile, and well-drained soil in full sun. Zones 6 to 10.

⌇⌇⌇⌇⌇⌇⌇⌇⌇⌇⌇⌇⌇⌇⌇⌇⌇⌇⌇⌇⌇⌇⌇⌇⌇⌇⌇⌇⌇⌇⌇

Bouteloua curtipendula, or side oats grama grass, is named in honor of Claudio Boutelou (1774–1842), a Spanish agriculturist who wrote about plants and farming. This charming grass is native to most of the United States, and has been introduced to most of the few states where it is not native. The common name refers to the oat-like, purplish spikelets that are arranged along one side of the inflorescence. The flowers stand above a two- to two-and-a-half-foot clump of gray-green leaf blades. They make great cut-flower additions to summer bouquets and then are great in dried arrangements. For years I've grown this grass in a rock garden setting because the plants prefer full sun, and seem to grow with more of a flourish

Bouteloua curtipendula

when sited in a moderately alkaline soil, rather than acidic. This is a great grass for naturalizing. It is also drought tolerant. The foliage turns golden-brown in the fall. Cut back for winter and propagate by careful division or by seed, the better method. Zones 5 to 9.

Bouteloua gracilis

Bouteloua gracilis [*Chondrosum gracile*] is best known as blue grama grass; its other, more descriptive, common name is mosquito grass, but it could just as appropriately be called eyelash grass. This is a densely tufted grass with light green foliage, very fine in texture, and plants are usually well under two feet tall. The flowers appear from late June to September, sticking out in a curved line from the tip of each flowering stem. They have a red tint that slowly fades to a straw color. Some say the spikelets look like mosquitoes clinging to the flowers, hence the alternative common name. They do beautifully when dried for winter bouquets. These grasses look great when used as specimens or when massed in the garden surrounded by other desert-like plants. They prefer full sun and a slightly acidic, light and sandy soil. Propagate by seed. Zones 5 to 9.

Brachypodium sylvaticum, the slender false brome, is included in this list not as a potential ornamental but as a rising pest. It's a European grass that escaped from cultivation and because it naturalizes so well, it easily takes over most areas with broadcast seed. The Nature Conservancy warns: "Don't take a chance with this grass! It creates monotypic stands in open grassland and forested habitats, and has been rapidly expanding its range in Oregon's Willamette Valley. It could likely spread into Washington, Idaho, and northern California!" The genus *Brachypodium* is derived from the Greek *brachys* for "short," and *podion* "foot," in reference to its short (or sometimes non-existent) pedicels or stems. Zones 5 to 9.

Brachypodium sylvaticum

Briza media

Briza media, the true quaking grass or, as it's sometimes called, rattlesnake grass, has been grown in gardens for centuries; the earliest herbalists noted its charm and presence in monastery gardens. Thanks to the movement of the seedheads in the wind, it's called *zittergras* in Germany. The scientific name comes from the Greek *briza*, a type of grain, in turn derived from *brizein*, "to nod." (*Briza maxima* and *Briza minor* are mentioned in the chapter on annual grasses.)

The true quaking grass is a warm-season perennial, growing in open tufts with erect culms and medium green foliage about eighteen inches high. The grasses bloom with panicles of dangling translucent heart-shaped florets that resemble puffed oats, fairy lanterns, or, if your imagination has a darker bent, rattlesnake tails without the buzz! These seedheads move about in the slightest breeze because each is attached to the stem with a thin wiry pedicel. The seedheads are green at first, then turn a warm bronzy-tan as they ripen. These panicles rise twelve to eighteen inches above the foliage. As summer advances the seedheads begin to shatter and fall to the ground. At this time, cut the plants back to encourage new growth. Provide a good, well-drained but moist soil in full sun.

60

Propagate by division whenever your weather warrants. A cultivar called 'Limouzi' is rare in America but available from a few English nurseries. It's described in *The RHS Plant Finder* as an improved form that makes a clump of mid-green grassy foliage, with airy pendant spikelets that are green at first, then turn a rich harvest yellow by midsummer. This can be used as a winter annual in Zone 10. Zones 5 to 9.

Buchloë dactyloides

Buchloë dactyloides, or buffalo grass, is listed here, not as an ornamental but as a lawn grass, because it's been used to that purpose in our area for years. The color is gray-green and, according to Albert Spear Hitchcock (1865–1935), the author of the monumental *Manual of the Grasses of the United States*, "Buffalo grass forms, when unmixed with other species, a close soft grayish-green turf . . . and is one of the most important grain grasses of

Buchloë dactyloides

[the Great Plains]. The foliage cures on the ground and furnished nutritious feed during the winter. The sod houses of the early settlers were made mostly from the sod of this grass."

The scientific name is from *buchloë*, adapted from the Greek *boubalos*, or "buffalo," and *chloë*, from the Greek for "grass." Like a buffalo, this grass is tough. So at this juncture let me suggest that you search out the Brooklyn Botanic Garden's great handbook *Easy Lawns: Low Maintenance Native Grasses for Gardeners Everywhere*. In addition to the carex lawns discussed by John Greenlee, many fine suggestions are given for using true grasses to alleviate the watering and weeding of the usual American lawn. Zones 5 to 8.

Calamagrostis

Calamagrostis is a genus of grasses with more than 250 species, though few are important in the world of ornamental grasses. But while few, those important ones are among the most stellar grasses. The species and cultivars listed are magnificent grasses; the cultivar 'Karl Foerster' salutes the German horticulturist who brought ornamental grasses out of the Victorian cupboard and into the twentieth-century garden. The scientific name is from the Greek *kalamos*, or "reed," and *agrostis*, a genus of grasses that includes the beautiful annual, *Agrostis nebulosa*.

Calamagrostis × *acutiflora* 'Karl Foerster'

Calamagrostis × *acutiflora* 'Karl Foerster', commonly called feather reed grass, is a perennial grown for the great flower plumes. Originally Karl Foerster called the plants by the cultivar 'Stricta' but that has changed (the world of botanical nomenclature is, in itself, a full-time job). This cultivar is today named in his honor. The plants form a two- to three-foot arching clump of mid-green, shiny, fourth-inch-wide blades. In colder climates (such as my original Catskill garden) they

Calamagrostis × acutiflora

reach a height of four feet. Usually from May to June, depending on the climate, they produce four-foot plumes of upright flower spikes that are first green, tinged with pink-violet and reddish-bronze overtones. By late summer, the plumes bleach into a warm buff color. In my Asheville garden the original clay soil was amended with plenty of humus, and today these grasses are stars in the front border. Propagate by division in spring. Zones 5 to 8.

Calamagrostis × acutiflora 'Overdam', the striped feather reed grass, has white variegated foliage with a golden-yellow inflorescence. Personal experience tells me that this grass resents hot, humid summers and does better where nights are cool. Zones 5 to 9.

Calamagrostis brachytricha, or Korean feather reed grass, is a better bet for warmer

climate gardens. It flowers in September with plumes tinted a rich purple-red tone, the flowers lasting well into winter. It also tolerates some shade, and if without adequate water, shade is necessary. Propagate by division in spring or fall. Zones 5 to 9.

Calamagrostis brachytricha

Calamagrostis epigios, or reed grass, is a native of Eurasia and grows beautifully in the wet woodlands of the British Isles. Once as a child I was rather ill and for two nights a nurse came in to monitor my progress. To this day I remember the comforting sound of the rustling of the nurse's skirts, and when a light breeze blows through its leaves this grass has the same effect. Often grown for the flowers, this grass is worth having for the leaves alone. It does well with damp soil but adjusts to dry sites, even thriving in the heavy clay soil found in my

Asheville garden. This grass can seed about but never becomes a threat. Zones 5 to 9.

Chasmanthium latifolium

Chasmanthium latifolium [*Uniola latifolia*], northern sea oats, river oats, or wild oats, is one of our most beautiful native grasses, long admired in the trade and at home in many Southern gardens. They are rather tall and graceful perennials, with flat leaf blades and open panicles of compressed, flat spikelets that resemble oats, hence the common name. Even the English doyen of the garden, William Robinson, said of sea oats: "[It's] a handsome perennial grass from N. America . . . [and] a clump, placed in rich garden soil, gathers strength from year to year, and when well established is a beautiful object."

In moist soil height is often up to five feet, but only three to four feet on dry sites. The foliage is especially valuable because, while it turns from light green to a polished bronze at maturity, the panicles retain the color they had when picked, if gathered at any time during the ripening process. These same seedheads do not absorb artificial colors with ease so are usually offered as nature provides, not dyed in unnatural shades of fuchsia or violet. The genus is attributed to an ancient Latin name of a plant, and the species means "broad-leaved."

Grow river oats in pots, in the perennial border as specimen plants, along the woodland border, at streamside, or wherever a particularly decorative aspect is needed. The plants will seed about but it's a very easy chore to pick out unwanted seedlings or pot them up for a friend.

Luckily for the gardener, these grasses are not only drought tolerant, but do beautifully in shade, preferring a well-drained but evenly moist soil with added humus. Cut back in spring before the new growth appears. Propagation is by seed or division. Zones 5 to 9.

Cortaderia, as a genus, opens up a large can of garden worms. It's one of those plants whose entire fate for a century was quite possibly decided by one species, *C. selloana*, the infamous Pampas grass. It was a favorite of the Victorians and they planted it to such success, both in formal gardens and cluttered backyards, that when it arrived in America, it caught the public's fancy (especially when the plumes were used to decorate Jean Harlow's hotel suite or to fan Cleopatra in Hollywood films of the 1930s). By the end of World War II, seemingly every motel in the South had to feature giant clumps of this grass on either side of gates that beckoned travelers to a comfortable rest. The genus is from the Spanish *cortar*, "to cut," referring to the sharp, almost saw-like, edges of the leaf blades, which can inflict nasty cuts if the gardener is not wary when digging in the area.

Their demands are few: good soil, plenty of water, and full sun. Like many clumping grasses, over time they form tussocks of old stems that are unsightly. In England one of the methods used for control is to emulate prairie fires by screwing up several shoots of newspaper and making a small bonfire. Unless you are next door to the fire department, this is not the way to go. Instead, wearing heavy gloves, cut out the old growth by hand, close to the ground.

The following are some of the species and cultivars available today. While a few are said to be cold hardy in Zone 6, that really depends on how much the temperature plummets in your area and the frequency of snow as an insulating blanket for the roots.

Cortaderia jubata

Cortaderia jubata, pink Pampas grass, is similar to *C. selloana* but the flowers have a decidedly pinkish cast. I saw it blooming in Sissinghurst and on a wet afternoon, the plumes were decidedly procumbent but as the sun came out and warm June breezes blew, they soon dried and were a stunning addition to the perennial border. Plants can reach a nine-foot height and can endure a windy location. The plants are adaptable to a variety of soil conditions, including a wet site, and are known

for their tolerance to drought. One thing should be noted: This is an aggressive spreader and reseeds with ease in a warm climate.

Cortaderia richardii

Cortaderia richardii, or New Zealand Pampas grass, is a gracefully blooming grass quite unlike its more plume-like relatives. I first saw it in the Inverewe Botanic Gardens, about 600 miles south of the Arctic Circle, where the ten-foot-high inflorescences nodded like a parade of plumes. Zones 7 to 9.

Cortaderia selloana

Cortaderia selloana is the original Pampas grass imported from the plains and open slopes of South America, native to Argentina, Brazil, and Chile. It has long been a lawn ornament in much of America, and in sunny California is often seen in movies, especially scenes shot on golf courses. W.C. Fields can be seen in front of a magnificent Pampas grass in his hilarious 1930 short feature, *The Golf Specialist*.

When siting this grass remember that it's big and a mature specimen takes up a good deal of room. Soil should be fertile, with adequate moisture available (they do great when planted by—not in—well-watered soil), and as much sun as possible. As described above, cut the old tussocks back and if resorting to power shears, remember to buy a good set.

Cortaderia selloana

Propagation is by seed or by division. Zones 8 to 10. The following are a few cultivars:

Cortaderia selloana 'Andes Silver'
is a large Pampas—said to be more hardy than the group in general—bearing heavy silvery-white plumes, topping seven feet, and hardy even in Zone 6. Zones 6 to 10.

Cortaderia selloana 'Argentea', the
silvery-blooming Pampas, grows between nine and twelve feet high. Seed is available from Chiltern Seeds, which also offers a cultivar with rose-tinted plumes. Zones 8 to 10.

Cortaderia selloana 'Aureolineata',
the gold band Pampas, stays between five and six feet high, and bears foliage with golden-yellow variegations. Zones 8 to 10.

Cortaderia selloana 'Pumila', the
small Pampas grass, is for those gardeners with limited space. Barely topping six feet, the white plumes adding an additional foot, this is a great plant for a border feature or a specimen plant. Zones 7 to 10, but it's been known to survive a mild Zone 6 winter.

Cortaderia selloana 'Rendatleri'
grows between eight and nine feet tall and bears pink plumes. Zones 8 to 10.

Cortaderia selloana 'Silver Comet' is
an eight-foot stunner with white variegated foliage and white plumes. Zones 8 to 10.

Cortaderia selloana 'Sunningdale Silver' is a European Pampas grass cultivar
selected for the beautiful feathery plumes and the contained size when in flower. Zones 7 to 10.

Cortaderia selloana 'Pumila'

Cymbopogon citratus, or lemon grass, is necessary in every garden where exciting food is on the owner's menu. In December 2002, *The New York Times* ran an article by Marian Burros about, of all things, lemon grass. While touring Bangkok, she drove out into the countryside and everywhere she looked saw fragrant patches of this wonderful treat. And, she added, in Thailand the lemon grass is "fragrant and fresh," not like the rather thin, not too succulent, leaves usually found in American food stores and co-ops.

Lemon grass grows throughout Southeast Asia and, along with basil and kaffir lime leaves, is one of the ingredients that separates Thai cooking from the rest of the world. In Thailand lemon grass is called *takrai* and is found in every backyard garden.

A member of the same genus that provides the world with citronella, lemon grass has such fragrance and essential oils that the leaves are used to dispel gas. The dried leaves make a wondrous tea. The bottom three inches of the stalk are used, which almost resembles a bulb—but isn't. And in addition to the flavor for cooking, lemon grass is the source of the lemon oil used to scent cleaning solutions and soaps. According to Burros, farm women report that dogs chew the blades of lemon grass to settle sour stomachs. The plant may also have antibacterial qualities, but research has yet to be completed.

The grass rarely tops four feet in a pot but can go well over six feet in the tropics. For growing in a pot use a good potting soil and start with a six-inch pot, remembering to transplant to larger pots as the grass grows and when roots amble out of the pot's drainage hole. Fertilize once a month when plants are in active growth. The grass grows well in the heat of summer and by season's end should be ready for a gallon container.

Then when frost threatens, bring the grass indoors to a greenhouse or a sunny window, remembering that it cannot withstand the slightest touch of freeze.

Cymbopogon citratus

Lemon grass can be grown from a few stalks purchased in an Asian food store or a supermarket with imagination, but the "bulbs" must be fresh in order to root.

Lemon grass will keep in the refrigerator for at least a week and the leaves can be cut or stored whole in the freezer—and they will quickly thaw to be used in a grand dinner.

Cymbopogon nardus, or citronella grass, is another member of the lemon grass genus, originally a native of Southeast Asia and grown there commercially as a crop plant. Like lemon grass, the leaves have a marvelous scent of lemon and have been used for fragrance and for medicinal applications for centuries.

Using steam distillation, an essential oil is obtained that is a natural deodorizer, used in the manufacture of insect repellents, including candles and lotions. Avon's Skin-So-Soft contains this oil, and this particular product is especially valued for its insect-fighting abilities.

Like lemon grass, citronella is a clump-forming tropical perennial that can reach a six-foot height, with gray-green, flat blades on top of cane-like stems. As the plant matures, the clump increases its girth.

Propagate by dividing the clumps. Provide full sun and a good, moist, humus-rich soil. It's a perennial but needs a long hot growing season to really mature, and is not hardy beyond Zones 10 to 12.

Dactylis glomerata 'Variegata'

branches of the panicle. Striped orchard grass is the variegated form and one of the most beautiful. The green is the green of a Key lime pie and the white is nearly pure. The plant is a charming addition to any garden. The clumps will spread and eventually sprawl to make dense colonies. The flowers bloom as fluffy spikelets on foot-high stems and, while attractive, the full beauty is in the overall plant. Provide a good, moist, well-drained soil in full sun when growing it in the mountains, but in the rest of the South provide a bit of shade from the hot noon sun. Propagate by division in spring or in fall. Zones 5 to 7.

***Dactylis glomerata* 'Variegata'**, or variegated orchard grass (sometimes called cocksfoot grass), is a European native imported as a meadow and pasture grass that now grows wild in much of the United States. The scientific name is from the Greek *dactulos*, "finger," referring to the stiff

Deschampsia caespitosa, or tufted hair grass, is one of thirty-five species of *Deschampsia* found growing in both hemispheres, with at least three species native to the United States. According to the USDA, tufted hair grass has a broad ecological range and is especially useful for revegetation, particularly on disturbed sites at high elevations.

Deschampsia caespitosa

Their generic name celebrates Louis Deschamps (1765–1842) the French naturalist and physician of the late eighteenth century. The species means "growing in dense clumps."

This genus has some of the most beautiful grasses available, noted for their clouds of airy blooms that can become so thick they obscure the foliage below. You haven't seen anything as lovely as tree peony blossoms peeking through an airy thicket of tufted hair grass. Look for plants growing in meadows and at the edges of woodlands, usually in moist soil. They form dense tufts of foliage, usually under three feet high and often arching over to the ground, the leaves up to a half-inch wide. These cool-season grasses adapt to a goodly amount of shade. They are beautiful when planted as specimens, massed and planted in

drifts, or partnered with Japanese maples. It should be noted that these grasses generally do poorly in the southern part of Zone 9, so might not be the best grass choice if you live in that zone. They also don't appreciate winter chills. Propagate by seed or by division. Plants are evergreen south of Zone 7, and in most of the South. Zones 5 to 9. Notable cultivars include:

***Deschampsia caespitosa* 'Bronzeschleier'** is the largest of the hair grasses, its blossoms up to three feet high. This is a marvelous bloomer and desirable in any garden that can give it ample room. Zones 7 to 9.

Deschampsia caespitosa 'Bronzeschleier'

***Deschampsia caespitosa* 'Goldgehange'**, or gold pendant tufted hair grass, bears nodding golden-yellow flowers at heights up to three feet.

***Deschampsia caespitosa* 'Goldschleier'**, or gold veil tufted hair grass, bears nodding golden-yellow flowers on two-foot stems.

***Deschampsia caespitosa* 'Northern Lights'** was introduced in 1993 by Harlan Hamernik at Bluebird Nursery in Nebraska.

Growing low to the ground, the leaves have longitudinal stripes of creamy-white. This cultivar is grown for the leaves and not the blooms, which have yet to be described.

Deschampsia caespitosa 'Schottland',

or the Scottish tufted hair grass, has tufts of dark green leaves and blooms with spikelets held to a height of up to four feet. In my garden it's in full sun on a bank overlooking the front lawn and inspirers favorable remarks from all garden-loving passers-by.

Deschampsia caespitosa 'Tardiflora'

is, as the cultivar name implies, a late bloomer, with stems up to three feet tall.

Deschampsia caespitosa var. *vivipara*

is the proper title but 'Fairy's Joke' is the best name for this, one of the few truly delightfully named cultivars in the world of ornamental grasses. The varietal name means "live young" and refers to the plantlets that appear at the ends of the flowering stems in lieu of flowers and seeds. Sometimes the plantlets can be so heavy that the stem bends to the ground and the "joke" will root.

Deschampsia caespitosa var. *vivipara*

Deschampsia flexuosa [*Aira flexuosa*], or wavy hair grass, is found growing throughout much of the Temperate Zone from New Zealand to Norway. The plants bear tufts of the finest hair-like leaves and in summer bear open panicles of shining purple or silvery spikelets. This is a cool-season grass and probably will not do well south of Zone 8.

Elymus represents the rye genus of grasses, numbering some 120 species, usually found in the world's Temperate Zone. They are described as fine forage grasses and often part of native hay. The species with creeping rhizomes are great binders of the soil. The scientific name is from an old Greek name for a type of grain.

Elymus arenarius 'Glaucus'

[*Leymus arenarius*] is a cultivar of the European dune grass and sometimes mistakenly sold as *E. glaucus*; currently part of a name change to the genus *Leymus*, for now I'm staying with *Elymus*. The species means "growing in sandy places."

This is the famous blue grass that Gertrude Jekyll touted in her garden arrangements. She wrote in the 1900 book *Home and Garden* that the "...so-called silver thistle (*Eryngium maritimum*) would present a picture of rare beauty, especially if approaching the flowers of blue and silver there was a planting of the blue-leaved Lyme Grass (*Elymus arenarius*). I have no such stretches of sandy waste, but knowing how it will do in a place that is poor and dry, I grow it in the end of a shrub-clump, where a large Birch tree robs the ground, and where I think nothing but this fine handsome Grass would be likely to flourish."

I planted it between a variegated willow (*Salix integra* 'Hakuro-nishiki') and stone steps—the rain running over the mortar of the steps and adjacent wall giving the acid garden soil a small shot of lime.

This grass is a spreader, so in good receptive soil it can get out of hand. If that's your problem, grow it in pots, just to get that wonderful flash of steel blue. The plant grows up to three feet tall but the blades often gracefully bend to the ground. Blooms appear in high summer but are probably best cut off so they don't compromise the color of the grass. Provide an average soil, full sun to light shade, and, in the warmer parts of the Southeast, the plants never really go dormant. Zones 5 to 9.

Elymus canadensis

Elymus arenarius 'Glaucus'

Elymus canadensis, or Canadian wild rye, is a native of North America where it is usually found growing at the edges of river banks, on open ground, and in sandy soil, ranging from Quebec to southern Alaska, and south to North Carolina, Missouri, Texas, Arizona, and northern California. Height is up to five feet and spread to three feet.

This cool-season grass is a clumper, generally used as a cover crop and a food for wildlife. Even if plants are short-lived, it's a valuable ornamental because of the blue-green foliage and the attractive nodding blooms, very effective when picked for dried flowers and bouquets. Provide average, dry to slightly moist, well-drained soil in full sun; plants adapt to a wide range of soils. Propagate by seed or division. Zones 5 to 8.

Elymus magellanicus [*Agropyron magellanicum*], or wheat grass, possesses the bluest color available in today's grasses. While not common in the average nursery collection, it's now available from several Internet sources and well worth the search. This is a clumper with a one-foot height and spread, usually sold as the cultivar 'Blue Tango'. The blossoms greatly resemble the flowers of wheat, hence the common name. A native of

Tierra del Fuego, the one problem is the reaction of this grass to excessive summer heat and high humidity, so unless you live near the cooling breezes of the seaside, expect that the beauty will wane during the summer. It does beautifully in a pot and on my terrace sat on the edge of the wall in a terra cotta Greek-style amphora, where it was one of the stars of the potted garden. That is until a raccoon knocked the pot over the edge when I was out of town; when I returned it was too late to rescue the grass. Wheat grass prefers a moist, well-drained soil and full sun, but in the Deep South provide dappled shade from the intense summer sun. Propagate by seed or by division. Zones 6 to 8.

Elymus solandri hails from New Zealand, a grass that, according to Chiltern Seeds, forms dwarf mats of striking metallic silver-blue leaves and is great for planting on a sunny bank. Named after Daniel Carl Solander (1733–1782), a Swedish naturalist who served under English botanist Joseph Banks on the *Endeavour* expedition of Captain James Cook. Recently renamed (as I warned, the *Elymus* genus is under continued renaming), this grass was once called *Elymus rectisetus*. The leaves grow in pale-green to blue-green tufts and bear very attractive flower heads, with up to ten spikelets, and individual florets having long slender awns. This is only available by seed (I found it in the Chiltern Seeds 2003 catalogue).

~~~~~~~~~~~~~~~~~~~~~~~~~~~~~~~~~~~~

Eragrostis is a worldwide genus known collectively as the love grasses, consisting of about 250 annual and perennial grasses with little forage value to livestock but with several species that excel as ornamentals. They are named from the Greek *eros*, "love," and *agrostis*, a type of grass.

Eragrostis curvula

Eragrostis curvula, the weeping love grass, makes a three-foot clump of narrow light-green blades that gracefully arch from the center like a fountain. Originally native to the mountainous regions of Tanganyika, in 1927 it was introduced to America as an ornamental, then again in 1934, this time as a forage crop for abandoned or eroded land in the Southeast. Thin, dark green leaves up to an eighth of an inch wide, the blades darken to a beautiful bronzy-red after a hard freeze. The spikelets arch out on three-foot stems, starting as a blackish olive-purple and aging to a light gray. This grass grows beautifully in the southern parts of California, Nevada, and New Mexico. The species grows on most well-drained soil but prefers a sandy mix and does not resent

Eragrostis curvula

Eragrostis elliotti

poor fertility. This species is often used as a ground cover and can be planted to provide a haven for ground-nesting birds. Propagate by division or by seed. In parts of Africa this species is viewed as a threat, but recent research points to a new cultivar, known as *Eragrostis curvula complex* or 'Consol', a leafier plant that is more acceptable as a ground cover. Zones 5 to 9.

Eragrostis elliotti, the blue love grass, is a three-foot high, three-foot wide native bearing fine textured blades, blooming in early summer with a long-lasting fluffy inflorescence. The fall-blooming flower clusters rise up on three-foot stems, making a cloud of airy tan. This is a great border or specimen plant, not to mention spectacular when massed. Provide a good, well-drained soil in full sun. Propagate by division or by seed. Zones 7 to 9.

Eragrostis spectabilis, the purple love grass, is described by Mary Evans Francis in the 1912 *The*

Eragrostis spectabilis

Book of Grasses. She wrote, "As the sunlight of early morning falls across the meadows laced with threaded dew, the flowering-heads of this grass glisten with an intense colour which is reflected in each crystal dewdrop that gems the spikelets. In dry fields, where the September sun has burned to a golden brown the shorter growth of grasses, ripening panicles of Purple Eragrostis, like a reddish purple mist, often cover the ground . . . still noticeable during autumn." This is a clumping warm-season grass that makes tight mounds up to eighteen inches high and about as wide. The summer-blooming panicles consist of red to purple spikelets and, toward the end of summer, the foliage acquires highlights of red. Provide a well-drained soil in full sun. Propagate by division or by seed. Zones 5 to 9.

Eragrostis trichoides, the sand love grass, is a cool-season grass that grows as a clump of medium green foliage, up to two feet tall and spreading about the same. Nodding panicles of showy, amethyst pink spikelets open in late July and bloom into fall. They are so bountiful the stems often bend under their weight. Provide a moist, well-drained, preferably sandy soil in full sun. If it's in a hot dry place, weekly waterings are welcome. A cultivar known as 'Bend' has even heavier bloom. A great plant for west Texas. Propagation is by division or by seed. Zones 5 to 9.

* * *

Erianthus represents some twenty species of grasses found in both tropical and temperate regions of the world. The genus has recently been changed from *Erianthus* to the sugar cane genus or *Saccharum* by some botanists, but this change will take a bit of time to accomplish, so for now, I'm sticking to *Erianthus*. (Hardy sugar cane, however, is listed as *Saccharum arundinaceum*.)

Mostly warm-season grasses, most of them are very attractive in autumn, with colors ranging from light orange to red to purple. They have no known pests or diseases. The scientific name is from the Greek *erion*, or "wool," and *anthos*, "flower," referring to the wooly glumes, or tiny bracts that appear on the flowers.

Erianthus contortus, or bent-awn plume grass, is a native of the Southeast, making its home in moist sandy pinelands or open ground from the coastal plain, north to Tennessee and Oklahoma and south to Florida and Texas. The foliage is a handsome blue-green changing to red and purple with the frosts of autumn. The clumps reach a height of two to three feet with the flowers standing two to three feet above the leaves. The flower spikes begin as a silky purple and fluff out with age. The species name refers to the bent awns. The dried flowers are great for bouquets. Prefers a well-drained soil in full sun but will tolerate dryer soil and light shade in the South. Zones 7 to 9.

Erianthus giganteus, or sugar cane plume grass, is a native grass said to be one of the dominant grassland plants in the Southeast before the arrival of man. Often confused with other wetland grasses, upon maturity this grass sports a large and conspicuous, wooly plume-like inflorescence. The reed-like stems reach a twelve-foot height, growing from a basal clump. The long, flat leaves are three-fourths of an inch wide, rough to the touch. Blooms are a terminal fifteen-inch inflorescence opening as pink but turning white, and full of awned spikelets, the awns about an inch long. These grasses flower in September and October. In nature these grasses grow in wet soils, including bogs and ditches, but easily adapt to sand and clay. Propagate by division or by seed. Zones 7 to 9.

Erianthus ravennae

Erianthus ravennae [*Saccharum ravennae*], ravenna grass, is another European import with tall plumes reminiscent of Pampas grass, but slightly less showy. The leaves make a lovely fountain effect of light green that, after the frosts of autumn, turns golden-brown, with various hints of orange, brown, and purple. A bit of thought is also necessary for its placement because this plant has a tendency to dominate almost any setting. The flower plumes appear in late summer and can easily reach a height of fourteen feet, while the grassy clumps are from three to five feet wide. In mountain gardens, leaving the foliage in place until spring will help to protect the root system. These grasses make a

great hedge, or excel as specimens. According to a few Web sites, this grass, when young, provides food for water buffaloes in the Far East. Provide a moist, well-drained, and fertile soil in full sun. Propagation is by division or seed—although when using seeds it usually takes two years to get any blooms. Zones 6 to 10.

Festuca comes to mind when seeding or reseeding the lawn because this genus is a prime constituent of fine-textured lawns. With about 300 species now listed, fescues are grasses primarily of the Temperate Zone and range from diminutive rock garden types well under a foot high to *Festuca gigantea*, a grass over five feet in height with one-sided panicles of green spikelets. The genus is derived from the Celtic word *fest*, meaning "pasture."

Festuca 'Blue Glow'

Festuca amethystina, or tufted fescue, is a southern European native, a clump-growing grass with thin leaves that are usually more blue than green. Plant height is a little over a foot, with the flower spikes rising another foot or more above the foliage. This grass and its many cultivars are especially suited for the rock garden, massing in the border, or as specimen plants dotted here and there for their delightful appearance and color. Individual plants can be set out in various designs, too. They are primarily cool-season plants so they prefer a cool spot in full sun. Most of them do not mix with hot, humid weather. Propagate by division and in some cases by seed. Zones 5 to 9.

***Festuca amethystina* 'Klose'** is named for a German nurseryman, Heinz Klose. This is a compact grass up to eight inches tall, bearing very fine olive-green leaves and, according to John Greenlee, doesn't turn brown in hot summer climates. The flowers are not very showy, so grow this cultivar for the overall effect.

***Festuca amethystina* 'Superba'** has fine-textured, weeping, blue-green foliage and grows about a foot tall, bearing pretty pink spikelets in spring.

Festuca californica, the California fescue, is a cool-season, clumping grass that in nature grows on dry ground, thickets, and open woods, up to an elevation of 5,000 feet, ranging from Oregon to California, and west of the Sierra Nevada. The one- to two-foot leaves are up to three-eighths of an inch wide, and grow from a dense basal tuft. Bluish-green panicles bear many spikelets that mature to a golden brown color. This plant is an exceptional ground cover growing in good, moist, well-drained and fertile soil, in full sun or partial shade. Zone 8.

Festuca gigantea, the giant fescue, does best in shaded locations where the three-foot, V-shaped leaves, up to three-fourths of an inch wide, often twist about, revealing their undersides. Flowers appear in midsummer and rise about eighteen inches above the foliage. Not very common in the trade, it's worth searching for through the various

Festuca gigantea

seed societies, because it's a stellar grass when planted in a wooded spot. I grew it shaded by a grove of azaleas where it prospered for many seasons until it suddenly disappeared during an extremely wet and chilly winter. So be sure the site where you plant this grass is well drained. This is not a grass for a sunny site. Propagate by division or by seed. Zones 5 to 9.

Festuca glauca

Festuca glauca [*Festuca ovina* 'Glauca'; *Festuca ovina* var. *glauca*] is, for color, one of the best of the

blues. Perfect for the rock garden, the stiff needle-like blue foliage and spikelets of a light green with a purple tinge appear above the foliage from late spring to early summer. One cultivar, 'Solling', never flowers at all. Not only do they look great next to rocks, but they are perfect container plants. They also do well as edgings or massed in the border, but when using these grasses as ground covers, space them no more than ten inches apart. Although tolerant of drought, they tend to die out in the center and should be divided or replaced every two years. They are cool-season grasses that tend to go dormant, looking quite forlorn during the summer, until the weather cools again. They can be cut back in fall or early spring. They need average soil, dry to medium wet, but any soil must be well drained. Remember foliage may decline in hot, humid summers. Zones 5 to 10.

Festuca glauca 'Elijah Blue'

Festuca glauca **'Golden Toupee'** is a very well-named plant, with a height from eight to twelve inches, producing tight clumps of finely textured, bright yellow, evergreen foliage. This grass is a charmer in small containers. It's a good idea to divide this grass for optimum growth. A good winter annual. Zones 5 to 8.

Festuca glauca **'Elijah Blue'** is a compact hunk of a beautiful bright blue, growing about ten inches tall and about fifteen inches wide, making a good ground cover or an imaginative edging for the garden or pathway. Full sun to partial shade. Zones 5 to 8.

Festuca mairei, the Moroccan fescue or maire's fescue, is one of the larger fescues used in gardens; its narrow, flat, fourth-inch leaves can grow up to three feet tall. The color is a glossy pale gray-green. The spring-blooming flowers are not very showy. Often used to control slope erosion, it makes an attractive specimen plant or massed in the border. Provide a moist, well-drained, fertile soil in full sun. Thanks to its mountain heritage, this grass is tolerant of heat, drought, and poor, but well-drained soil, but can develop rust. Propagate by seed or division. Zones 5 to 9.

Glyceria maxima var. *variegata*, striped or variegated manna grass, originally hails from Eurasia where it inhabits the sides of streams and generally wet surroundings. The genus is from the Greek *glukeros*, or "sweet," as the seeds of some species are sweet to the taste. Manna grass is a dense spreader with half-inch-wide, ribbon-like blades up to six inches long that wrap around two- to three-foot culms. The foliage is striped green with pink in early spring, the pink changing to white and yellow as the summer advances. It's an effective ground cover for wet areas and does well growing in pots, but in all situations the wandering rhizomes should be contained. This grass likes a moist, rich soil, or shallow water, in full sun, and does well in hot climates as long as there is plenty of water. Propagate by division. Zones 5 to 8.

Glyceria maxima var. *variegata*

Gynerium sagittatum, or uvagrass, is a one-species genus with its origins in the Old World tropics and, amazingly, often found in gift shops where its fifteen-foot (or more) culms are topped with large silky plumes—often three feet in length—usually dyed bright colors and sold as dried flowers. The scientific name is from the Greek *gune*, for "female," and *erion* for "wool," referring to the woolly spikelets. The species name refers to arrows (*sagitta* is Latin for "arrow") because Native Americans used the stems for

Gynerium sagittatum

arrow shafts. This grass can top forty feet in height and has leaf blades over six feet in length and almost three inches wide.

Hakonechloa macra, a classic woodland ground cover, is sold by nurseries in its most common variegated form but the species has been as rare as the proverbial hen's teeth. There is but one such species, originally at home on the wet rocky cliffs and mountains of Japan's main island of Honshu, where it's called Japanese forest grass or Hakone grass (named for Japan's Mt. Hakone), in addition to being called *urahagusa*. The elongated culms hold graceful leaf blades of an almost perfect green and the plants are reminiscent of bamboos. The scientific name refers to the plant's home, combined with *chloa* from the Greek for "a grass."

Last year a giant poison ivy vine, some three inches in diameter, fell away from the ancient red oak where its thread-like roots held it in place all the years that I've gardened on this property. Once gone, a whole new vista opened to view, a perfect place for ferns and some elegant grasses. At the same time I found one Hakone grass at a local nursery and quickly brought it home.

There I planted it in front of two awesome oak roots and this grass immediately became a winner where it soon reached a height of about three feet, the long stems topped with eight-inch blades. And when it bloomed in early September, with open arching panicles sporting a few attractive spikelets, I knew the species was, at least to me, finer than the various cultivars.

Hakone grasses are very shade tolerant and they slowly spread, becoming a marvelous ground cover, their charm often enhanced when planted at the edge of a small pool or next to a large rock. Remember, unlike many grasses, these plants need a good moist soil, rich with organic matter; exposure to full southern sun will easily burn the leaves. In Japan these grasses are often grown in decorative pots as houseplants or set about the

garden in special places as accents. Propagate by seed and by division. Zones 5 to 9.

Hakonechloa macra 'Albovariegata'

***Hakonechloa macra* 'Albovariegata'**, the white variegated Hakone grass, is like the species, but in this cultivar the green foliage bears fine longitudinal stripes of white. It is said to be more tolerant of Southern heat than the other cultivars. Height is up to three feet.

***Hakonechloa macra* 'All Gold'** is new to cultivation but upon finding a source, remember that all-golden yellow blades need partial shade and moist soil, especially in the South. It was found in the Kowaguchi area of

Hakonechloa macra

Hakonechloa macra 'All Gold'

78

Japan by Dan Heims of Terra Nova Nurseries. This cultivar is best summered in a cobalt blue pot that overwinters in the greenhouse.

Hakonechloa macra 'Aureola'

Hakonechloa macra 'Aureola' is the cultivar usually offered by nurseries, with the blades entirely striped with wide or narrowing variegations of yellow and green. This is a shorter plant than the species and growth is usually about a foot high. The blades arch out into garden pathways like a wave of color. It's also a slow grower. Then in the fall, the leaves become burnished with reds and maroons. The leaves will burn in hot sun but lose much of their color in moderate to deep shade.

Helictotrichon sempervirens, or blue oat grass, is a member of a large grass genus with species located around the world, but in our gardens only blue oat grass has achieved ornamental status. These grasses are usually found on dry hillsides, among rocky outcrops, high meadows, and along the edges of woodlands. They are named from *helictos*, or "twisted," and *trichon*, referring to the awn, which is twisted. The species name is from the Latin for "evergreen," pertaining

to the foliage, which is evergreen in warm winter climates. In Asheville we cut it back to the ground in late winter.

Grass height is between two and three feet with a two-foot spread. The leaves are about a half-inch wide. The blooming spikelets, on three-foot stems, are a light buff or brown, but the leaves are a beautiful blue, with the blue tones intensified by exposure to sun. Provide a well-drained soil, ranging from dry to medium moisture. Rust fungus is a problem in areas of high humidity and heat and, as with many plants that want well-drained soil, crown rot is evident when these grasses are set in poorly drained or wet soil, especially clay.

In our garden blue oat grass is perched on the edge of the garden wall, next to a pink honeysuckle, so the colors act together like a garden watercolor—at least for a few weeks in the year. This grass also excels in the rock garden, looking spectacular when posed against a line of carefully chosen stones. Zones 5 to 8.

Three cultivars are available: 'Saphirsprundel' (also called 'Sapphire' and 'Sapphire Fountain'), which has steely blue foliage and a resistance to rust; 'Pendula' with a nodding

Helictotricon sempervirens

inflorescence; and 'Robust', reputed to be the best of them all for rust resistance.

Hystrix patula [*Elymus hystrix*], or bottlebrush grass, is so aptly named—frankly, it's curious why some plants get great common names and others do not. This species is a most attractive grass of the Eastern American woodlands and received its name because the blooming, awned spikelets lined up on the stem look exactly like a laboratory bottle-brush waiting to clean a test tube or two. In Greek *hystrix* means "hedgehog" (or European porcupine), which refers to the

Hystrix patula

resemblance of the seedhead bristles to hedgehog quills. This is a native grass, one of four species, with the others in California (*Hystrix californica*), New Zealand, and the Himalayas. In America it's found growing in dry or moist woods from Nova Scotia and Quebec down to Georgia, Oklahoma, and North Dakota.

Grass height is from two to three feet with an eighteen-inch spread. The spikelets open as green but quickly change to tan and last throughout the summer into fall. With the arrival of autumn winds and rains, the flowers shatter. If gathering for bouquets, remember to cut as soon as the spikelets are open or they will fall apart. Provide a good, dry or medium wet, well-drained soil. They also want open shade. In Asheville they are often found at the edge of the woods, well within city limits, and in my Catskill garden the plants actually did well in clay soil. Propagate by seed. Zones 5 to 9.

Imperata cylindrica, or cogon grass, when mentioned in a room full of horticulturists, environmentalists, and grass-lovers, is tantamount to unfurling a red flag in front of an ill-tempered bull. Today, it's ranked as one of the ten worst weeds in the world—and that's saying something. According to A. S. Hitchcock in his *Manual of Grasses*, around the 1950s this species was introduced into Florida as a forage grass and as a packing material. At that time it was quickly spreading, especially because of its strong creeping rhizomes. Today it's classed as one of the most serious weeds of dry lands in Florida, throughout the Southeast, and west to eastern Texas. According to the National Park Service this grass ". . . can invade and overtake disturbed ecosystems, forming a dense mat of thatch and leaves that makes it nearly impossible for other

Imperata cylindrica

plants to coexist. Large infestations of cogon grass can alter the normal fire regime of a fire-driven ecosystem by causing more frequent and intense fires that injure or destroy native plants. Cogon grass displaces a large variety of native plant species used by native animals (*e.g.*, insects, mammals, and birds) as forage, host plants and shelters." The scientific name is in honor of Ferrante Imperato (1550–c.1631), a pharmacist from Naples who studied plants and animals.

Amazingly enough, one cultivar, *Imperata cylindrica* 'Rubra', grown for over a century in Japan and known by the cultivar name of 'Red Baron' in the United States, appears to be quite harmless and to have a reasonably good deportment since it spreads slowly. But John Greenlee warns that some of the seedlings seem to

be prone to mutation, again becoming aggressive spreaders, so you should be careful of plants propagated by tissue-culture. Also, remove any plants that revert to green.

The twenty-inch leaves grow straight up; they are green at the base and red at the tips, with the color increasing as the summer temperatures rise. Plants rarely flower. They also seem to prefer a mildly alkaline soil. While a great ground cover, mine grows at the edge of a stone wall so if they do spread, they're brought up short. Japanese blood grass makes a great pot plant. Provide a moist soil in mostly full sun, granting some shade from the noon sun in the Southeast. Zones 6 to 9.

Imperata cylindrica 'Rubra'

Koeleria glauca

Koeleria glauca or blue hair grass hails from Central Europe to Siberia where it grows in sandy meadows and open conifer forests. The genus is in honor of G. L. Koeler (1765–1806), a botanist who specialized in grasses. As the species name implies, this grass bears bluish foliage. Basically a grass for cooler areas, I mention it only for the mountains of Georgia, North and South Carolina, and West Virginia. The height is about eighteen inches with a twenty-inch spread. It's a compact grass growing in dense clumps and does its best on poor but well-drained soils. A weak, cool-season grass, it's best as a winter annual. Zones 6 to 8.

Melica altissima, or the Siberian melic, is another grass I include for those gardening in the cooler parts of the Southeast. This cool-season native of Central Europe grows in woodland settings and resents hot, humid summers, so isn't a great choice once you come down from the mountains. The genus name comes from *melica*, an Italian name for a kind of sorghum (*mel* is "honey"), most likely from the sweet juice in some species.

Siberian melic forms a loose tuft of glossy green leaves about three-fourths of an inch wide and eight inches long. The showy spikelets bloom as a narrow panicle hovering about two feet above the leaves. These spikelets vary from white to a light purple and cling to the stems like papery grains of rice that rustle in the slightest breeze. This grass is best at the back of the border where flowering plants look great when massed. They will naturalize in a woodland garden. This grass needs a moist, well-drained, humus-rich soil. Propagation is by seed or division. Zones 4 to 8.

Melica altissima 'Atropurpurea', or purple melic grass, bears deep purple spikelets that fade with age. Zones 5 to 8.

Melica altissima

Melica ciliata

Melica ciliata, or hairy melic grass, is another import, this one from Europe and northern Africa. A cool-season grass, the gray-green leaves are about a fourth of an inch wide and up to a foot long, growing as loose tufts of foliage about a foot high. In early summer the showy rice-like spikelets appear as fluffy white panicles that fade and shatter with summer heat. Propagation is by seed or division.

Milium effusum 'Aureum' has two equally relevant common names, Bowles' golden grass and golden wood millet. The first honors E. A. Bowles (1865–1954), one of the great gardeners, a kind and gentle man whose life spanned two centuries. His garden at Myddleton House is still open to the public and originally included a separate area devoted to botanical misfits called "The Lunatic Asylum." The genus is from the old Latin name for millet. *Milium* is an American native (native to the Old World, too) and Hitchcock, who chose his words with care, described the species as: "A handsome grass, sometimes cultivated as an annual." This particular cultivar is a loosely clumping cool-season grass that opens up in spring with intensely yellow blades that fade to yellow-

green as spring comes to a close. The flowers appear on weeping sixteen-inch (or so) stalks that gracefully bend to the ground through the end of June. If your garden is cool enough to support this grass, it's a stunning accent, especially in a woodland setting. Provide a rich, moist soil in light shade. Propagation is by division, as the bright golden color doesn't always come true from seed. Zones 6 to 9.

Miscanthus as a genus is a giant, not only for twenty-first century gardens but the nineteenth and twentieth as well. If you collect old garden books, as I do, you'll know that gardeners from Mrs. C. W. Earle to William Robinson to Graham Stewart Thomas all grew ornamental grasses, especially miscanthus, and gave them high praise. But back in the early days when these grasses were first introduced from Japan and other parts of Asia, they were included in the genus *Eulalia* (named for Eulalie Delile, a botanical artist) and not *Miscanthus*—that name came later. *Miscanthus* is taken from the Greek *mischos*, or "pedicel," and *anthos*, "flower," because the flower spikelets are on tiny stems, or pedicels.

One of the worst plant pests in the Southeast is the typical species, *Miscanthus*

Miscanthus sinensis 'Variegatus'

sinensis (see page 86). Finally, this grass is not to be confused with another formidable grass pest known as Japanese grass or eulalia (its scientific name is *Microstegium*), an annual colonial grass that spreads rapidly, grows in the shade, and is now overtaking many lawns and gardens in the Southeast.

Miscanthus Blights

Just when you thought it was safe to grow grasses in the garden! After all, everybody knows that *Miscanthus* is one of those rare genera considered trouble free. Now two problems have sailed onto this plant horizon.

The first is the *Miscanthus* mealy bug. Here's a small, soft-bodied, white, wooly insect that settles down between the clasping leaf sheath and the grass stem, where it begins to suck at plant juices. A heavy infestation can stunt plants, resulting in bunched foliage and contorted flowers.

The second problem is much worse: a rust fungus that begins as isolated reddish-brown spots on the foliage—spots that grow, meet, and eventually merge, causing the death of the leaf.

As these are both newly reported conditions, the potential development of controls may still be on the back burner. But there are still solutions available to the knowledgeable gardener.

The first cure for a problem with rust funguses is to make sure there's plenty of air movement and that your grasses are not under undue stress. And mealy bugs are very susceptible to insecticidal soaps. Finally, never leave any plant trash—including diseased material—around the garden. A clean garden is a healthy garden.

The *Miscanthus* Cultivars and Species

The various *Miscanthus* grasses can remain in place for many years, gradually forming a bigger and bigger circle of growth. Except in the Deep South, they require little or no fertilizing, are reasonably

Miscanthus sinensis 'Variagatus'

drought resistant, with special care consisting of cutting off last year's growth and spent flowers before next spring's new growth begins. You can overlook that chore, but the new growth doesn't effectively hide the old until well into spring. Just remember that as the clumps enlarge, the centers usually die back and eventually the plants must be divided and replanted. The very tall varieties of miscanthus may need some staking as they grow, especially if your springs are wet and cloudy. The flowers generally open in late summer and range from shining silver to robust tan to stunning reddish-purple.

Care should be taken when handling the leaf blades, as most of them have sharp edges that can easily cut a human palm, not to mention finger joints. When working with these grasses (and many other species), wear stout gloves.

Finally, these grasses offer interest to the gardener throughout the year, acting as seasonal bridges as plants come into full glory and other plants wind down for the season. They make great background hedges for various perennial gardens, look great with roses, brighten up mixed borders, and generally improve most gardens.

Drying Miscanthus Plumes

When it comes to drying the flowers of the various miscanthus grasses, in the Southeast there's plenty of time for these floral plumes to mature and open. But back in nineteenth-century England, Mrs. C. W. Earle wrote in her charming 1899 book *More Pot-Pourri From A Surrey Garden:* "The two Japanese grasses, Eulalia Japonica variegata and zebrina, do not throw up their flower panicles here quite early enough to come to perfection, But I learnt last summer that if the cane containing the flower (this is easily distinguished by feeling a certain fullness near the top) is picked and brought into the house, the grass will dry; it should then be peeled off, and the feathery panicles will display themselves. They make a pretty and refined winter decoration, and are just the right size to mix with the red-berried pods of Iris foetidissima."

Miscanthus giganteus [*Miscanthus floridulus*], or giant miscanthus, giant Chinese silver grass, giant eulalia grass, Japanese silver grass, and Amur silver grass, is a clumping, warm-season, deciduous grass and the largest of the *Miscanthus* species. There is a great deal of discussion about M. *giganteus* and M. *floridulus* being the same or being different species, using minute examination of the spikelets to verify a difference. In the words of Chon Day when he drew that great *New Yorker* cartoon about a girl who replied, after being told by her parents to eat her vegetables, "I say it's spinach and I say the h*** with it!"

In a Southern garden this grass can reach a height of fourteen feet and a mature plant can easily provide enough two-inch culms to be cut as stakes and guarantee support for dozens of drooping perennials. Medium green leaves, up to an inch and a half wide, and almost three feet long, arch out from these sturdy culms, the culms almost resembling bamboo—in Japan they're used to make various kitchen utensils. In the South, as fall waits in the wings, eight- to twelve-inch-long flowering plumes appear on top of stalks that rise another two feet above the foliage. Then with

Miscanthus giganteus

frost, the leaves get stained with tints of burgundy and rust-red, and as leaves finally fall, you get a great garden "sculpture" for the winter months. In my garden, as the lower leaves brown and fall away, I finish the job and use the now denuded stems as garden interest of their own.

Provide a fertile, moist, well-drained soil in full sun. Propagate by division or seed. Zones 4 to 9.

Miscanthus sacchariflorus, or silver banner grass, is a native of China, Korea, and Japan. This grass has the potential for being a great colonizer because its spreading rhizomes reach out in all directions. The foliage reaches

Miscanthus sacchariflorus

six feet high, held aloft by stout culms. The medium green leaves are about three-fourths of an inch wide and about ten inches long, changing to a lovely orange-brown with the touch of frost. The flowering plumes appear in August, standing two or three feet above the foliage. This grass is especially fond of moisture and can actually survive in shallow water. Zones 5 to 8.

Miscanthus sinensis, Japanese silver grass or eulalia grass, is a dangerous grass. Before we list its impressive cultivars, heed the following warning: Grow the species with extreme care or perhaps don't grow it at all. *Miscanthus sinensis*, introduced by nurseries, and still being sold as a popular ornamental grass in the United States, can easily seed about and become a rampant weed. In Western North Carolina, this grass has infested the roadsides of both interstates and backwoods lanes. In some areas of the country warnings appear that miscanthus is a fire hazard and burning grasses have been reported to produce flame heights of thirty feet! I've walked in the far backwoods of Western North Carolina, on roads where the only cars belong to teenagers looking for a place to hang out with their peers, and the areas along the ditches are infested with this miscanthus.

Miscanthus sinensis spreads by seed and by its underground roots or rhizomes. The grass grows on a variety of sites, but prefers a moist, well-drained soil, hence its penchant for roadside growing.

Hand-pulling of these grasses is not always successful because the root fragments left behind will sprout again. I have used a glyphosate herbicide to good effect, but the plant must be in active growth.

Miscanthus sinensis Cultivars

The following is a short selection of *Miscanthus sinensis* cultivars available today at nurseries and better garden centers throughout the Southeast. These cultivars are presumably safe to grow. I have grown many miscanthus cultivars over the years and the only problem seedlings I've found—in and

Miscanthus sinensis

around Western North Carolina—are seedlings of the species *Miscanthus sinensis*. Zones 5 to 9.

Miscanthus sinensis 'Adagio' forms a small, tight clump of arching narrow-leaved blades, standing about two feet high and flowering in late August. In our garden it grows in a small bed that rises about two feet above a meandering path, so upon passing, you can fully appreciate this plant's charms.

Miscanthus sinensis 'Cabaret' has a place of honor in our large garden overlooking Kenilworth Lake. During the mid-1970s Dr. John Creech and Sylvester March collected 'Cabaret' and 'Morning Light' in Japan. It's a shame it took so long for two such beautiful plants to reach the gardening public. This is a stellar cultivar, with wide, ribbon-like foliage that is creamy-white at the center and lined with wide green bands at the edge of the leaf. At maturity, the height is said to reach nine feet. My plant is in its second year and is only up to five feet. It blooms in late September. Propagate by division.

Miscanthus sinensis 'Flamingo' is a lovely cultivar, especially valuable because of the rose-pink color of the blooming plumes. The color has been likened by some English commentators to that of a rich claret and the comparison is perfect. The plant height is between five and six feet and the blossoms appear in late summer. This is a beauty! Propagate by division.

Miscanthus sinensis 'Gracillimus', or maiden grass, is another of the timeless miscanthus cultivars that have graced American and European gardens since Victorian times. Introduced into England in 1888, here is how Graham Stuart Thomas described it: "The leaves are very narrow and the sheaf of stems reaches

Miscanthus sinensis 'Gracillimus'

about 1.5 m (5 ft), giving a most graceful dainty effect, the perfect antidote to solid clumps of hydrangeas." If called upon to choose one grass and one grass alone for any future garden, my choice would be this.

Miscanthus sinensis 'Little Kitten' is an aptly named cultivar because, although it has all the punch and robust energy of a typical miscanthus, this is a dwarf form rarely growing higher than two feet with an eighteen-inch spread. The creamy-white flowering plumes appear in August (touched with hints of pink and red), rising above the plant to thirty inches, and lasting well into winter. The dwarf size lends itself to pots and larger containers, not to mention edging a walkway or border.

Miscanthus sinensis 'Morning Light' is a stunning grass that does beautifully as a specimen plant or massed at the back of the border. Here is another cultivar that no garden should be without. The culms stand erect for about two feet, then the blades arch out in all directions, like the most graceful of fountains. The V-shaped (in cross section) leaves have a white mid-vein, and are edged with a narrow band of white, with thin stripes of green in between. When viewed against the setting sun, it's superb. This late-flowering cultivar has creamy-pink flowers.

Miscanthus sinensis 'Morning Light'

Miscanthus sinensis 'Nippon' is another cultivar especially suited for the smaller garden or for a container. The height is between four and five feet. The fall color is a good orangey-red, with the flower plumes standing two to three feet above the leaf-tops.

Miscanthus sinensis 'Puenktchen', or little dot (English translation) zebra grass, is an important addition to the cultivar list because of its tolerance of summer heat and high humidity. The height is between three and four feet, with the flowering stalks rising three feet higher. The dark green, finely textured leaves have zebra striping consisting of golden-yellow bands at four-inch intervals. The foliage turns a light brown or tan after frost. Basically a clumping grass, it does spread a bit with wandering rhizomes, but still keeps its shape. Provide an average, well drained, but moist soil in full sun to partial shade; in too much shade, the plant flops.

Miscanthus sinensis 'Purpurescens', flame grass or purple silver grass, is another grass choice happier in the mountains than down on the plains. But the marvelous autumn color, a brilliant orange-red, makes it a perfect choice in whatever garden will provide its needs. The leaves, which range in size from a fourth to a half inch wide, form three- to four-foot clumps. In late July the showy silver plumes appear, remaining to provide stark contrast to the autumn foliage tinted by frosts. Zones 7 and 8.

Miscanthus sinensis 'Puenktchen'

Miscanthus sinensis 'Silberfeder', or silver feather maiden grass, is one of the taller cultivars, with grass blades reaching up to a height of five to six feet and the blossoms standing another three feet above that. The flowers appear in mid-August and are a lovely blend of silk and silver.

***Miscanthus sinensis* 'Strictus'**, or, as it's commonly called, porcupine grass—a nickname based on the stiffly upright growth of the culms and leaves—is very effective when used as a specimen or planted in groups. The leaves are banded just as with zebra grass, but in this cultivar the spiky quality of the leaves creates a different look. Pinkish flowers appear in late October.

Miscanthus sinensis 'Strictus'

***Miscanthus sinensis* 'Variegatus'** arrived in England around 1873 and has graced English and American gardens ever since. As cultivars come and cultivars go, the lovely white variegations on this beautiful landscaping plant are still the best around. Writing in *Perennial Garden Plants*, here's how Graham Stuart Thomas described this grass: "A perfect companion to *Hibiscus syriacus* 'Blue Bird'. The flowering plumes appear in mid-September. If you have water in your garden plant a few of these grasses so they cast their reflections throughout the daylight hours." I've seen this grass stand up to the heat and humidity of a St. Louis summer and would never have a garden without its graces. In our garden two clumps of this grass are set off by the shorter form of Joe-Pye-weed and purple beautyberry (*Callicarpa bodinieri giraldii* 'Profusion').

***Miscanthus sinensis* 'Yaku Jima'** is a catchall name for several smaller forms of *M. sinensis*, usually growing less than five feet tall. The showy reddish flowers stand about eighteen inches above the leaves, appearing in mid-September. This is a great choice for the small garden.

***Miscanthus sinensis* 'Zebrinus'** is another cultivar that goes back to the nineteenth century. The gracefully arching leaves are not striped but dashed with horizontal bands of a butterscotch-yellow variegation. As the weather warms for summer, you can see the new grass blades, green at first but with slowly emerging variegations, spreading out on the leaf as it grows. Flowers are large and showy, giving an added plus to a truly beautiful plant. Plants easily reach a height of six feet. The leaves turn brown with the first touch of frost.

A few other cultivars with the zebra influence include 'Kirk Alexander', named for the Asheville

Miscanthus sinensis 'Zebrinus'

landscape designer who found this seedling as a shorter and more compact form of 'Zebrinus', and 'Little Nicky', another dwarf variety of zebra grass, perfect for the small garden since it never tops a height of five feet with a three-foot spread.

Miscanthus transmorrisonensis, evergreen maiden grass or Formosa maiden grass, is a native of Taiwan that arrived on the nursery scene after being collected by the Morris Arboretum. According to Chiltern Seeds, this beauty was found at an elevation of 9,500 feet back in 1979. Three- to four-foot tall tufts of green foliage spread in all directions to make a clump of foliage up to eight feet wide. Beginning in July, this grass is topped with six- to seven-foot spikes of attractive creamy-white plumes, and the plants continue to flower well into fall. Not only is this grass effective in the garden proper, it does well planted in tubs. Provide a moist, fertile soil in sun or light shade. These grasses resent long periods of drought. Propagate from seed. From Zone 8 south the foliage is evergreen. Zones 7 to 10.

Molinia, or moor grass, represents a small genus of European or Eurasian grasses, including one species, M. *caerulea*, that has made a major mark on the world of ornamental grasses. The genus is named in honor of J. I. Molina, an early student of the flora of Chile.

Molinia caerulea, or purple moor grass, is a densely tufted grass that forms a low fountain of foliage. The medium green leaves are a fine texture, up to eighteen inches long, and very narrow.

During the summer of 2001, I toured various Scottish gardens, including the world-famous Edinburgh Botanic Garden. After walking through the main gate, to the left a carefully tended bed of plants rose up a slight slope along the walkway. It was devoted to some twenty plants of purple moor grass, not a cultivar but just the plain old species, and, from the overall design to the beauty of the grasses, it was enviable on all counts.

Most of the moor grasses bear flowers on long stems and sometimes reach a height of seven feet. They are warm-season grasses of easy culture, and bring excitement to the garden for at least nine months of the year. When winter arrives, the seeds and leaves of moor grasses go crashing to the ground, not to reawaken until spring. In the mountains provide full sun, good soil, and plenty of moisture. In hotter areas, these grasses need partial shade and plenty of water. Zones 5 to 8.

Molinia caerulea

90

Molinia caerulea ssp. *caerulea* 'Variegata'

Molinia caerulea ssp. caerulea 'Variegata' is another favorite grass that is featured in most of my lectures dealing with garden design because it not only looks great in spring, but the look carries through to fall, and then to early winter when it looks like a Fourth of July sparkler, in shades of brown instead of brilliant neon tones. The variegated foliage forms a neat, compact mound of great charm. Then when the flowers appear, not only the leaves are variegated but the stems and panicles give the impression that all have been banded with a brush of light yellow paint. The only problem is the slow maturation rate of the plant—it takes at least three seasons for the show to begin. Propagate by division in the spring. Zones 5 to 8.

Muhlenbergia, a genus collectively (but improperly) known as deer grass, is a widely varying group of great looking ornamental grasses, generally from Mexico and the southeastern United States. They are called muhly for short, the genus having been named after G. H. E. Muhlenberg (1753–1815). He was the third son of a Lutheran minister, a self-taught botanist, personally naming about 150 plant species, and called by his contemporaries the American Linnaeus.

The muhly grasses represent about 125 species and many should be stars on the grass horizon but, so far, get short shrift from many nurseries. Thanks to native plant societies, they are slowly getting the attention they deserve. Muhly grasses are tough, love the heat, and if not adaptable as perennials to a particular climate, respond well when grown as annuals.

Muhlenbergia species

Muhlenbergia capillaris [M. *filipes*], the hairy awn muhly (the species designation means "hair-like" or "delicate," referring to the flowers), is described by Hitchcock as a tufted perennial bearing purple panicles, in a color best pictured by imagining a purple haze on the horizon, with the Sons of the Pioneers humming a cowboy ballad in the background. Until it blooms in mid- to late August, the plant is a nondescript clump of blades, about thirty by thirty inches, but when the bloom-tipped culms are adorned with a topdressing of cloud-like wisps of reddish-purple, you will be in awe.

A native grass of the moist pine barrens near the Atlantic coast of North and South Carolina, Florida, Georgia, and parts of Mississippi and Texas. Provide full sun to partial shade. In late winter or early spring cut the blades almost to the ground to remove the browned leaves and spent flowers. Zones 7 to 10, but not good in the hotter areas of Zone 10.

Muhlenbergia capillaris

Muhlenbergia dumosa, a muhly grass first described by America's grass maven, A. S. Hitchcock, found growing in the canyons and valley flats from southern Arizona to Jalisco, Mexico. The species name *dumosa* means "of bushy habit."

Muhlenbergia dumosa

My first introduction to this grass was in 1994 when JC Raulston (of the great arboretum in Raleigh, North Carolina), featured it in his North Carolina State University Arboretum Plant Distribution, a collection of plants given to North Carolina nurserymen to help spread the world's plant wealth around.

"A stunning ornamental—a grass I first saw in the gardens at Yucca Do Nursery in the fall of 1992 while on a Texas lecture tour," said Raulston. "The texture and form were unique and exquisitely beautiful—I felt it to be the most beautiful new ornamental I saw in 1992. [It's a] clump-forming (no aggressive runners) grass with coarse bamboo-like stems which emerge from the ground to a height of five feet and arch out from five to seven feet, like a graceful fountain of finely divided, almost gossamer-like pale green foliage."

And if you can't provide the necessary heat for winter survival, find a great container and grow this plant for the glories of the summer in your area. Zones 8 to 10, but not good in hotter areas of Zone 10.

Muhlenbergia emersleyi, or bull grass, is a native grass that was originally found in rocky woods and ravines from Texas to Arizona

92

and Mexico. The plants boast clumps of graceful evergreen leaves that vary between an eighth- and a fourth-inch width and a two-foot length. Reddish flower plumes appear in the fall and easily top four feet.

A cultivar called 'El Toro' was collected in southeastern Arizona, where it's found in dense colonies. This blue-green grass is smaller and more compact than deer grass (*Muhlenbergia rigens*), growing up to three feet tall and about three feet in width. Dark purple flower spikes appear in late summer. This is a very drought tolerant grass, doing well in full sun or partial shade. Zones 6 to 10.

Muhlenbergia lindheimeri

Muhlenbergia lindheimeri, or Lindheimer's muhly, is at home in Texas and northern Mexico where it grows on rocky slopes, often in calcareous soils, along the edges of creeks, and on open plains. It's another clumping grass with blue foliage and pale gray floral spikes on two- to two-and-a-half-foot culms. Cut in section the leaves are V-shaped, of a soft blue, usually about eighteen inches long. Taking a cue from its home grounds, provide this grass moist, well-drained, fertile soil in full sun. It will grow in clay soil, as long as the clay is amended with organic material. Zones 7 to 9, but not good in wet Zone 9 climates.

Muhlenbergia lindheimeri 'Autumn Glow' is a lower growing plant up to two feet in height and up to four feet in diameter. Dense, fluffy tufts of plumes give an appearance of a dwarfish version of Pampas grass.

Muhlenbergia pubescens, or the Mexican muhly, originates in central Mexico on rocky cliffs and high up on canyon walls. The species name refers to the down-like covering on the leaves. Like most muhlys, this grass is a clumper that produces blue-green blades, up to three-eighths of an inch wide and usually about a foot long. The downy leaves have a weeping habit, with pale lilac-colored flowers that bloom in September and stand about three feet above the ground. The foliage turns a reddish-purple when frosts threaten. Provide well-drained, fertile soil, and full sun. If you have clay soil it must be amended with plenty of humus and, if necessary, with drainage tiles underneath the soil to guarantee perfect drainage. Propagate by seed in spring or division in the fall. Zones 9 and 10.

Muhlenbergia rigens, or deer grass, is a cool-season grass growing in clumps; it is heat tolerant and actually flourishes in times of drought. Described by Hitchcock as being "slender and stiffly erect," the spike-like two- to three-foot panicles are greenish-gray in summer, turning a pale buff as winter enters the

Muhlenbergia rigens

Oplismenus hirtellus, or basket grass, is one of the few grasses well suited to be a potted plant (an excellent choice for a hanging basket), and an outdoor plant in warm climates. The genus, from the Latin word *oplismenos*, meaning "armored," refers to the sparse but spike-like blooming panicle. The species *hirtellus* means "somewhat hairy," an unfair designation, as the hairiness is so slight as to be nonexistent and only visible in the blossom. This grass arrived in England from New Caledonia back in 1867, although it has also been claimed to be a native of Mexico and Texas. It's a creeping, freely branching grass with thin, lance-shaped leaves, one to three inches long, and green spikelets with purple awns, which bloom on and off throughout the year. The cultivar 'Variegatus' is usually found in the trade, a variety that has white and pinkish-purple striped leaves that almost sparkle, as long as the plants get plenty of sun and water. Basket grass is used as a ground cover,

garden scene. Their colors go beautifully with cactus gardens and water features. Originally found growing in elevations up to 7,000 feet on open ground, gullies, hillsides, or open forest from California down to Mexico. Provide a moist, well-drained, fertile soil in full sun or partial shade, this grass adapts to alkaline and saltwater conditions, so it's especially adapted to oceanside plantings. The Native Americans used it to make baskets. Propagate by seed or division. Zones 7 to 9.

Muhlenbergia rigens 'Nashville' is a smaller version of common deer grass, reaching a height of about two feet with the same width. While dormant in winter, this grass displays purplish spikes with tan undertones that eventually fade to a light tan. Zones 7 to 9.

Oplismenus hirtellus

especially in moist ground and medium to deep shade. Propagate by rooted cuttings. Zone 10.

⌣⌣⌣⌣⌣⌣⌣⌣⌣⌣⌣⌣⌣⌣⌣⌣⌣⌣⌣⌣⌣⌣⌣⌣⌣⌣⌣

Oryzopsis hymenoides, or Indian rice grass, is found in every state west of the Mississippi River, and is the state grass of Nevada and Utah. During times of bad harvests the Native Americans of the Southwest ground the seeds into flour for bread. Beautiful in both the landscape of nature and of the mind, it was saluted in *The Grass Harp* by Truman Capote when he compared the sound of its dry leaves rustling in the wind to " . . . sighing human music, a harp of voices." It's known for its ability to reseed areas damaged by fire. The scientific name is from *oruza*, "rice," and *opsis*, "appearance," because of its resemblance to true rice. The species name refers to the light, airy look of the grass.

A clumping, cool-season grass, Indian rice grass grows in very delicate-looking tufts, up to two feet tall and about two feet wide. The narrow, graceful leaves are about eight inches long. The flower stems are very thin and hold aloft open panicles of beautiful spikelets. This grass is often grown for the cut-flower market. Plants are usually dormant by June when they turn a lovely straw color. This grass also resents a too-rich situation, preferring dry, sandy soils in full sun. It will adapt to heavier soils but it will not live in heavy wet spots or shade. Propagate by seed and remember to follow instructions carefully, because Indian rice grass needs cold stratification of up to two months. Zones 7 to 9, but not good in hot, wet Zone 9 areas.

⌣⌣⌣⌣⌣⌣⌣⌣⌣⌣⌣⌣⌣⌣⌣⌣⌣⌣⌣⌣⌣⌣⌣⌣⌣⌣⌣

Panicum represents a genus of grasses that includes proso millet (*Panicum miliaceum*), a grain that is often grown for food and forage.

Nearly 600 species of annual and perennial *Panicum* grow in many different climates, ranging from deserts to mountains, and from swamps to forests. The common name of panic grass has nothing to do with sounding an alarm. Rather, it's from a Middle English word, *panik*, from the Middle French or Latin, in turn from the Latin *panicum*, referring to the panus or stalk that connects the panicle to the stem.

***Panicum amarum* 'Dewey Blue'** is a new variation on the common beach grass, called bitter panic grass and found growing along the coast from Connecticut to eastern Texas, even down to Cuba. This cultivar reaches a three-foot height and, although initially a clumper, it does spread with creeping rhizomes, hence its value as erosion control. The leaves are distinctly blue and plants grow about three feet tall. Airy flowers appear in the fall and, with the arrival of frost, turn a light beige color. Thanks to its ability to withstand salt spray, this is a great grass to plant along ocean property. The species name is the Latin word for "bitter." Provide a dry and well-drained soil. Zones 3 to 9.

Panicum clandestinum [*Dichanthelium clandestinum*], or deer tongue grass, was named by Linnaeus in 1753. This grass comes into its own when a light touch of frost covers the garden. Deer tongue is a native found growing in the wild throughout most of the Southeast, with the possible exception of Florida. It's a clumping, warm-season grass bearing short but wide, bright green, bamboo-like leaves about seven inches long, on culms usually up to thirty inches high. The species name is a nod to the creeping rhizomes just beneath the soil's surface.

And except on very poor soil, it's an aggressive spreader, as witnessed by the

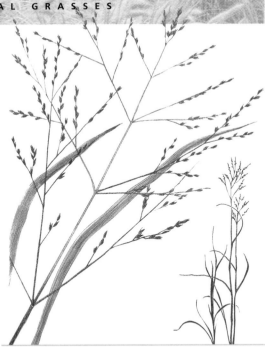

Panicum virgatum

warnings put out by the state of Hawaii: "In the past, often used for soil stabilization [but] not recommended due to its invasive nature [and] a problem in Hawaii, La Réunion, Australia, New Zealand, and South Africa." But when kept in bounds, its autumn foliage is most beautiful, the leaves tinted with subtle hints of red and golden-brown. Propagate by seeds or division. Zones 4 to 9.

Panicum clandestinum

Panicum virgatum, or switch grass, is one of the most valuable native grasses from the American prairies. The species name refers to the long and slender culms. It is found growing in the prairies and also around sites in open woods and brackish marshes from Nova Scotia and Ontario, Maine to North Dakota, and south to Florida, Nevada, and Arizona. While the original species was not really suited for the more formal garden, it's a natural for mass plantings or when used as a low screen to block an unwanted view. The open panicles are especially attractive when viewed against a dark background. The fourth- to half-inch-wide leaves are up to two feet long and clothe stiff culms. Plants can be up to seven feet high. The blooming panicles rise about two feet above the foliage and begin to flower in July, with airy spikelets at first having pink and red tints but

fading to tan. They make great additions to dried bouquets. This grass is simply magnificent in the fall after a touch of frost.

Switch grass will withstand poor drainage and flooding, growing with wet feet for weeks without visible discomfort, so it makes a great erosion control for banks prone to seasonal flooding, and tolerates salt spray. It also withstands some light shade but begins to bend if there's too much. Propagate by seed and by division in spring. Zones 5 to 9. The following are just a few of the many cultivars being brought to market.

Panicum virgatum 'Hänse Herms', or red switch grass, is shorter than the species, reaching a height of about three feet, or a bit more. Purple-red highlights begin to appear on the leaves as the summer heats up and by fall they're a reddish-orange, finally turning to a gray-brown. The spikelets mature to a whitish gray.

Panicum virgatum 'Heavy Metal'
bears stiff, metallic blue leaves growing in a tight
clump, reaching a height of about three and a half
feet. The flowers rise about sixteen inches above
the foliage. I've had a clump of this cultivar in my
front garden for five years and every autumn, folks
who walk by comment on the beauty of this grass.

Panicum virgatum 'Heavy Metal'

Panicum virgatum 'Northwind' has
five feet of upright foliage, with over a two-foot
spread, that tolerates many soil conditions
ranging from downright dry to boggy. By late
summer finely textured yellow flower panicles
float over the foliage like an airy cloud of color
dots. The panicles turn beige as the seeds mature
and persist well into winter. Provide an average,
medium to wet soil in full sun or a bit of shade.

Panicum virgatum 'Shenandoah', or
red switch grass, begins with green leaves that
darken with tints of red as the summer heat
progresses, and by September are a burgundy
red. The plants are about four feet tall.

Pennisetum is a genus of about 140 tropical
species of annual and perennial grasses found
around the world. One species, called pearl millet
(*Pennisetum glaucum*), was probably cultivated in
Africa 3,000 to 5,000 years ago, then spread to
southern Asia. A few listed here are cultivated for
ornament and at least five species are adventive in
the Southeast. The generic name is from the Latin,
penna, for "feather," and *seta*, for "bristle," referring
to the plumose bristles in the spike-like panicles.

The flowers of this genus are, for the most
part, quite beautiful: elegant plumes that range in
color from silver-white to pink or red—and even
black. While a few are hardy in Zone 5, the various
species are treated as annuals in colder parts of the
country and for good reason. When grown in most
of the Southeast they become perennial grasses
and a few species soon become weedy and can be
landscape pests. This potential threat can be
remedied by removing flower heads before they
mature to prevent unwanted seedlings.

Pennisetum alopecuroides [*Pennisetum
japonicum*], or fountain grass, is a Chinese import,
a warm-season grass that looks like a green
fountain. The leaves, up to half an inch wide,
grow up to thirty inches long and form a dense,
weeping mound. The very showy flowers appear in

Pennisetum alopecuroides

midsummer and last well into August. Like graceful foxtails, these blossoms, up to three inches wide and often ten inches long, emerge in colors ranging from creamy-white to light pink to tan. This grass works in mass plantings, in groups, as specimens, and in containers. Provide a good, moist, well-drained soil in full sun. While tolerating some shade, plants refuse to bloom without enough sun. Propagate by seed and by division in spring. Plants will reseed. Zones 6 to 9, but needs a winter chill to survive.

Pennisetum alopecuroides 'Cassian'

grows in a three-foot-high mound and bears light brown flower plumes. The leaves turn a brushed gold with the arrival of frost.

Pennisetum alopecuroides 'Hameln',

or dwarf fountain grass, has dark green leaves, narrower than the species, up to twenty inches long, with white flowers up to two inches wide and four inches long, maturing to a creamy tan. This is probably the oldest cultivar of the species and named for the German city, home of the Pied Piper. It's beautiful when massed or grown in a small group, or in containers. It's perfect for the small garden. Provide a good moist soil and try it in rock gardens or along the banks of creeks or ponds.

Pennisetum alopecuroides 'Hameln'

Pennisetum alopecuroides 'Little Bunny'

is the smallest of this line of cultivars, apparently a seedling of 'Hameln'. The plants are only eighteen inches high, blooming in August and perfect for the rock garden.

Pennisetum alopecuroides 'Little Honey'

was a sport of 'Little Bunny' that usually grows about a foot high when in bloom and just about eight inches high when in leaf. The leaves are longitudinally striped with white. Provide full sun in a good, well-drained soil. Zones 5 to 8.

Pennisetum alopecuroides 'Moudry'

[*P. alopecuroides* 'Viridescens'], or the black-flowering pennisetum, is a beautiful grass. It was not imported from New Zealand and named in honor of a native tribe (whose name is actually the Maori), nor was it, as rumored, a horticultural form found by the Cincinnati Parks Department. Seed actually came from the Baltimore city horticulturist, G. Moudry. While strikingly beautiful, it is extremely invasive. Upon ripening, the bristly seeds attach themselves to people and animals, not to mention the wind, and are soon invading your neighbor's lawn two doors down the street or your own perennial border. This grass is attractive enough for its foliage, but when in flower, sporting six-inch black plumes on eighteen-inch stems, it's almost worth letting them flower—even considering the trouble of cutting back those flowering stems before the seeds mature. And that's a job you *must* do!

Pennisetum 'Burgundy Giant'

is called a "horticultural selection" because nobody seems to know its exact parentage. Originally found as a chance seedling at the Marie Selby Botanical Garden in Sarasota, Florida, this is a monumental ornamental grass. A clumping warm-season grass, the leaves are up to an inch wide, up to a foot long,

Pennisetum alopecuroides 'Moudry'

Pennisetum caudatum, the white-flowering fountain grass, is another East Asia import that resembles *P. alopecuroides*, but the flower plumes bloom as creamy-white, are narrower in size, and fade to tan with age. Some authorities consider it a variety of that species. The species means "ending in a tail-like appendage," referring to the plumes.

Pennisetum incomptum [*P. flaccidum*], or the meadow pennisetum, is yet another Chinese grass, this time from northern China up to the Himalaya Mountains. An aggressive creeper, this warm-season grass bears blue-green leaves a bit wider than a fourth of an inch and up to eighteen inches long. They wrap around sturdy culms, reaching a final height of two to three feet. The flowers are purple-pink vertical foxtails that usually appear in June. They mature to a creamy white. The leaves turn a light yellow to tan with the touch of frost. In the landscape this grass is best for a large area, in addition to being a good candidate for holding the soil. A mass of this grass in bloom is quite beautiful. Provide a good moist soil in full sun to light shade. Propagate by seed or by division. Zones 6 to 9.

Pennisetum messiacum '**Red Bunny Tails**' fountain grass, is a really dwarf grass, to three feet, upright arching in form. The flowers are reddish black at emergence only, then dry to a tan color. Starting in early summer it sends up flower plumes that resemble the annual hare's-tail grass (*Lagurus ovatus*). It's a drought-tolerant plant that prefers full sun; in colder parts of the Southeast it is treated as an annual or moved to a protected spot for the winter. The species is named for a French city. Zones 7 to 9.

Pennisetum orientale, or oriental fountain grass, hails from Central Asia to the Caucasus Mountains to western India. It's a clumping warm-season grass desired by all who see it in

and rise on stout culms, making this burgundy fountain reach a five-foot height, the total effect being decidedly tropical. The blooms appear in midsummer, flowering as purple-red plumes that fade to creamy-white with age, arching about two feet over the foliage. Whether planted in groups or as specimens or in containers, this is one beautiful grass. Provide a good, moist, well-drained soil in full sun. Plants will also survive in coastal gardens if protected from the wind. 'Burgundy Giant' does not seem to set viable seed, so propagate by division. You can overwinter this grass in a greenhouse or protected area where temperatures stay above 40° F. Zones 9 to 10.

Pennisetum orientale

Pennisetum orientale 'Karley Rose'

top blue-green blades. Plants are three feet tall, the same in width, and more upright in form. Full sun. Zones 7 to 9.

Pennisetum setaceum

bloom because of the marvelous showy pink foxtails. Each are up to four inches long and half an inch wide, and arch out twelve to sixteen inches above the foliage. Remember, it takes two seasons for this particular grass to settle in, so be patient because it's worth the wait. Provide a moist, well-drained soil in full sun or light shade. Well-drained is the key with this grass as it hates wet feet. Propagate by seed or by careful division of older plants only, in spring. Zones 7 to 9.

Pennisetum orientale 'Karley Rose' is a long-blooming grass with a larger flowering foxtail than the species. Blooming from late spring to fall, the dusty-rose flowers

Pennisetum setaceum [*P. ruppelii* or *P. macrostachyum*], or fountain grass, hails from Africa and is usually treated as an annual in most of the Southeast. It's a lovely grass with attractive blossoms, all in the graceful form of a green fountain. Blooming from seed in the first year puts it firmly in that class of warm-season perennials that work as annuals where the winter can be cruel. The flowers can be picked for bouquets, but not after the seeds have ripened as they will quickly shatter. The clumps can reach a height between two to three feet, topped with those purple-pink racemes up to eight inches long and up to an inch wide. Provide a well-drained, moist, fertile soil in full sun, but the plants adapt to poorer soil as long as they have plenty of water. For all its beauty in areas warmer than Zone 7, be very careful because this grass will seed about and could become a potentially invasive pest. Propagate by seed. Zones 8 to 10.

Pennisetum setaceum 'Eaton Canyon' ['Cupreum Compactum', 'Rubrum Dwarf', 'Red Riding Hood'] is described by John Greenlee as a dwarf cultivar from Santa Barbara, California. It's almost identical to 'Rubrum' but grows only about thirty inches tall. This grass looks striking in a designer pot.

Pennisetum setaceum 'Rubrum'

Pennisetum setaceum 'Eaton Canyon'

Pennisetum setaceum 'Rubrum', or the purple fountain grass, has become a garden designer's delight in America. Even a "box store" with the poorest selection of plants often has this cultivar on display. But popularity is often the reason something becomes a cliché. This grass is popular because it's beautiful, especially when planted with colorful annuals. It's a clumping warm-season grass with burgundy leaves and red-purple foxtails forming four-foot

clumps (and just as wide); the flowers are up to a foot long and often an inch wide. This grass works when massed or used as a border or as a specimen, and looks great in a decorative pot. It tolerates some salt spray, making it a favorite with coastal gardeners. Provide a good, well-drained, moist soil in full sun. In hot summers the plants need water. To keep the same color when multiplying the plants, propagate by division in spring. Zones 9 and 10.

Pennisetum villosum [*P. longistylum*], or feather-top grass, is a perennial from Ethiopia that most catalogs list as a half-hardy annual. The species name refers to the blossoms, which are shaggy with long, soft hairs. Feather-top is rather floppy in appearance because the magnificent flowers become quite heavy, especially when capped with dew. If picked

Pennisetum villosum

Phalaris arundinacea 'Picta', or, as it's often called in England, gardener's garters, has graced American gardens for many years. It's acquired a host of common names, including ribbon grass, whistle grass (when a blade is held between the fingers and given a hearty blow, it emits a piercing whistle), painted grass, and, in a spelling variant, gardener's gators. Some older references call it reed canary grass because the seeds were once used as bird food, and probably still are. If one grass is found growing by an old and forgotten country garden, this is it. The genus translates as "shining," referring to the shiny seeds, and the species means "reed-like." The cultivar name means "painted." When the narrow lanceolate leaves emerge they have a

before they open entirely, they can be dried for bouquets but readily shatter with the slightest bump. They are beautiful when picked as fresh flowers. The creeping foliage, propelled by wandering rhizomes, reaches two feet in height, the soft leaves and stems clothed with short silky hairs. The large blossoms are up to five inches long and up to four inches wide, and start to bloom in July: a silky-green when new but aging to a creamy white. In the warmer parts of the Southeast, this grass can be mowed. Provide a good, moist, well-drained soil in full sun or light shade. Plants tolerate just about everything, even salt spray.

But—and it's an important *but*—this grass can be a pest where it's warm enough to winter over, and is not legal in Florida. The blossoms shatter and the wind easily propels the seeds, which use those silky hairs as sails. Zones 9 and 10.

Phalaris arundinacea 'Picta'

Phalaris arundinacea 'Picta'

pink and white variegation that quickly changes to longitudinal stripes or ribbons as the leaf expands, hence the reference to garters.

In her chatty and informative 1901 book, *Old Time Gardens*, Alice Morse Earle wrote: "We children used to run to the great plants of Striped Grass at the end of the garden as to a toy ribbon shop. The long blades of Grass looked like some antique gauze ribbons [and] were very modish for dolls' wear, very useful to shape pin-a-sights, and very pretty to tie up posies."

The leaves are up to an inch wide and about seven inches long and often flop over by the beginning of summer. If summer heat is too severe and water in short supply, the leaves often scorch, but the grass can be cut back about six inches from the ground and new foliage will

appear. Beware of wandering rhizomes, as this grass can quickly conquer places where it's not wanted. An easy grass, hence its survival in so many gardens, it will adapt to just about any soil but prefers a moist, well-drained soil in full sun to partial shade. This grass will even adapt to wet feet and will grow in several inches of water. Propagate by division in spring. Zones 5 to 9. New cultivars are continually being introduced.

Phalaris arundinacea 'Feesey's Form', or, as it's sometimes called, 'Strawberries and Cream' is a cultivar with white-striped leaves blushed with pink, the pink fading as the season progresses. In early July flowers appear in soft white panicles, maturing to brown. This grass tolerates standing water so is not a good choice for the dry garden. It also resents too much heat.

Phalaris arundinacea 'Luteo-Picta' is a spreading warm-season cultivar a lot like 'Picta' but the variegations are a pale golden yellow instead of white. The variegations begin to fade by late summer.

Phalaris arundinacea 'Woods Dwarf' or dwarf gators is a compact form of 'Picta' with shorter leaves (about seven inches long), and usually growing about fifteen inches tall, spreading slowly.

Phragmites australis, or common reed grass, is present in European fossil evidence as one of the oldest grasses known. It grows on all the continents of the world and has different uses in different cultures. In England, it has been used to thatch roofs and to make fences and even some types of furniture. In our American West, Native Americans used this most adaptable plant to make

Phragmites australis

of this grass in bloom is a stunning sight indeed. The spikelets emerge as a purplish red but slowly change to a medium tan in the fall.

This grass is best in areas where the reclamation of land is of primary import and there is plenty of room for spread. If in the home setting, it must be contained, using drainage tiles or a similar barrier. If bordered by a lawn, the mower should do the trick.

***Phragmites australis* 'Variegatus'** is a much shorter grass, usually topping in at eight feet. The leaves are striped with bright yellow. It looks great reflected in a small pond but is probably best grown in a pot.

Poa is a large genus with close to 500 species, the most notable member—at least to most Americans—being Kentucky blue grass or *Poa pratensis*. The plants, while not unattractive, are mainly used for planting lawns. *Poa* is the ancient Greek name for grass.

Poa costineata, or Australian blue grass, grows as a clump-forming grass up to two feet tall with a two-foot spread. The leaves have a glaucous underside and are silvery green on top, so when in motion they actually sparkle. In spring an airy panicle rises about a foot above the foliage, remaining throughout the summer. Provide full sun to partial shade in well-drained soil, but this grass will flop in too much shade. Plants will tolerate both drought and some moisture and are great in the border or the rock garden. Zones 8 to 9.

lattices for adobe huts, rugs and mats, shafts for arrows, and even portable nets. While often too large and demanding for the ordinary garden, it makes a visual statement all year-round and reed grass will do very well in a damp and poorly drained site that supports little else. It grows in highway ditches throughout the eastern part of America and, finally, has the distinction of holding much of the New Jersey marshlands together. The genus is the Latin word for "reed" and the species means "from the south." This grass is known as a pioneer plant and, like cattails, it fills in shallow ponds until they eventually become dry land.

Common reed grass bears bluish-green leaves, up to an inch wide and a foot long, emerging from stout culms. A healthy grass can reach a height of eighteen feet, but usually measures about twelve. The attractive blooming plumes rise two feet above the foliage, and a field

***Rhynchelytrum nerviglume* 'Pink Crystals'** [*Melinis nerviglume*] is a perennial

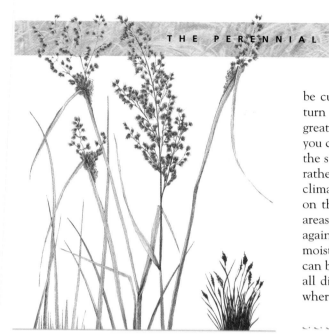

Rhynchelytrum repens

African grass usually grown as an annual. Height is between twenty and twenty-four inches, the leaf blades being a bluish-green. This grass was named a Plant Select Winner in 1998. The emerging flower heads first appear about a foot above the foliage and consist of three- to four-inch fuzzy racemes, beginning as a beautiful reddish-pink and maturing to a creamy white. Requirements are full sun and a moist but well-drained soil. It's an excellent grass for containers but Southern growers should be aware that is a potential pest where it's a perennial. Zones 8 to 11.

Rhynchelytrum repens [*Melinus repens, Rhynchelytrum roseum, Tricholaena rosea*], champagne grass or Natal ruby grass, is an African import usually listed in seed catalogs as a half-hardy annual. In most publications it's a tender tropical that can flower in the first year of growth. The foliage grows about two feet tall with glossy blue-green leaves about five inches long, which often flop. The flowers arch out over the foliage and bloom over a long season, only to

be cut down by frost. The reddish-pink plumes turn to soft silver and these blossoms make a great cut flower. Although they shatter with age, you can dry them for indoor bouquets if you pull the stems out of the leaf sheath when gathering, rather than breaking them. If grown in a mild climate this grass is evergreen, flowering off and on throughout the year, but in exceedingly dry areas, the grass is dormant until rain begins again. Provide a good, fertile, well-drained but moist soil in full sun. In the right spot, this grass can become invasive, the seeds blowing about in all directions. This is not, of course, a problem where winters are colder. Zones 9 and 10.

Saccharum is the genus of the crop that feeds America's sweet tooth, sugar cane (*S.*

Saccharum arundinaceum in bloom.

officinarum). Some forty species are native to the Tropics, extending into the Temperate Zone. The genus is from the Latin *saccharum* (*saccharon*), or "sugar," because of the sweet juice. These are all warm-season grasses, grow in clumps, and produce beautiful plumy flowers.

Saccharum arundinaceum

Saccharum arundinaceum, or hardy sugar cane, is a somewhat hardy member of the family and, like many in the genus, a really big grass. It can easily grow ten feet high and ten feet wide. The stout culms produce long gray-green leaves with a distinct white midrib and serrated edges that can easily cut an unwary hand. A native of China, this giant clumper can easily take over the average garden. Then just when you get accustomed to its size, the purple-pink flower plumes appear in late September to early October, rising another two to three feet above the leaves. Finally, for the winter garden, the blades turn a lovely tan color and twist about at their tips like party favors for the New Year. It occasionally seeds about in Southern gardens but seedlings can be easily removed before they start getting big. Last year we had a Zone 6 winter in Asheville and the mature clump of this grass survived with ease, but two seedlings perished. Provide just about any garden soil in full sun. Zones 6 to 10.

Saccharum officinarum, sugar cane, can be grown in most gardens as a tender tropical treated as a half-hardy annual. The culms are up to two inches in diameter, and while they can reach heights of up to twenty feet in the Tropics, in backyard America six to eight feet is the norm. The flowers are fluffy panicles resembling the plumes of Pampas grass, but rarely bloom in cooler climes. Where it's warm enough these grasses are dramatic and quite in style with today's contemporary garden styles that salute the tropical look. And it's a tough act to follow at parties when you cut sugar cane into sections and everybody gets a taste. These grasses prefer a very fertile, moist soil in full sun. Once established they are somewhat drought tolerant. Propagate by seed, division, or rooted cuttings from cane sections (see *Arundo donax*). Zones 9 and 10.

Saccharum officinarum 'Pele's Smoke'

Saccharum officinarum **'Pele's Smoke'** and **'Violaceum'** are two cultivars that are almost identical, having purple stems with smoky purple foliage. The shiny culms have distinct cream-colored bands at the nodes. A quart-sized clump set out in spring after the frost threat has passed will be six feet tall by summer's end. Hunter Stubbs, the chief horticulturist at Asheville's Richmond Hill Inn, was the first gardener in our area to use this plant in one of his Victorian inspired gardens, and people talked about it all summer long.

Saccharum ravennae see *Erianthus ravennae*.

Schizachyrium scoparium

Schizachyrium scoparium [*Andropogon scoparius*], little bluestem, broom beard grass, wiregrass, or prairie beard grass, the state grass of Nebraska, is found in every state except those on the West Coast. Like big bluestem, this grass turns golden reddish-brown in the fall and is worth growing for that reason alone. You will often see little blue in abandoned fields and along roadsides where, during the 1930s, it was planted for soil conservation. This clump-forming, fine-textured grass is also valuable for forage. And it's a great grass for naturalizing. The small purple flowers are beautiful as cut flowers and in dried arrangements. The culms can grow from two to five feet tall, but usually measure in at three feet, with the light green blades up to eighteen inches long. The leaves have a coating of silky hairs and the floral spikes emerge from July thorough September, opening up to brighten the autumn sky when sunlight shines on their silky fibers. The genus means "dressed in silk." Provide almost any well-drained soil from perennial border to open field, in full sun. Propagation is by seed and by division. Zones 5 to 9.

Sesleria is a genus of about thirty grasses from Europe, often growing in a mountainside setting. Cool-season grasses, their foliage is often more pleasing than their flowers, especially with their long, smooth, pale blue-green leaves. The grass was named in honor of Leonardo Sesler, an eighteenth century Venetian physician who owned a botanic garden. Zone 5 to cooler Zone 9.

Sesleria autumnalis

Sesleria autumnalis, or autumn moor grass, hails from eastern and northern Italy up to Albania. This grass is upright in habit, growing to two feet tall. The narrow, bright green leaves are about a foot long. In warm climates the flowers bloom in late spring, but in colder areas, the blooming is in the fall, hence the species name. The flowers are six-inch-long cylindrical spikes, emerging purple-black with white silky stamens. They mature to brown. Provide a good, moist, well-drained soil in full sun to partial shade. These grasses grow well between trees that provide high, open shade. They will also adapt to slightly alkaline soil. Propagate by seed or by division. Zones 5 to 9.

Sesleria caerulea, or blue moor grass, is a clumping cool-season grass with attractive two-toned leaves that are a dark blue-green above and silvery beneath, many of them turned to give a glittering effect in a breeze. The flower clusters are small, about a fourth of an inch wide and less than an inch long. They emerge a purplish hue and mature to golden-tan. Prefers a good, moist, well-drained soil in full sun or partial shade and needs plenty of water in hot climates. Propagate by seed or division. Zones 5 to 9.

Sesleria nitida [*Sesleria glauca*], or gray moor grass, is a native of central and southern Italy and the Swiss mountains. The leaves are long and silvery gray on the top and pale green beneath, pointed at the tips. Dark brownish flower clusters are held above the foliage in early spring. Adaptable to most well-drained soils in sun or partial shade.

Setaria palmifolia, palm grass, Malaysian palm grass, or New Guinea asparagus, has traveled to our shores from Asia and India after being introduced into Jamaica as an ornamental. In Southeast Asia this grass grows in damp, shady situations at altitudes from sea level up to 6,000

feet. About six years ago, I received seed of palm grass from a correspondent in the Canary Islands. I had been looking for this particular plant for many years because several old books dealing with greenhouse plants called it a magnificent and beautiful addition to the conservatory. The genus is from the Latin *seta*, or "bristle," referring to the bristle-like inflorescence.

A few references cite that the seeds are used as a substitute for rice, but usually it's an ornamental plant. The emerald green blades are plaited, about twenty inches long and about two and a half inches wide, growing on stems up to six feet tall. A variegated form, variety *niveovittatum*, was introduced in 1868 by Messrs. Veitch and Son of England. This type has long, deep green leaves striped with white and just a touch of pink—but in all my searches, I've never found it. There is also a form *Setaria palmifolia* var. *rubra* with deep red stem sheathes at the base of each blade.

Setaria palmifolia

Narrow flower stalks appear in summer and the plants are very adaptable regarding location, taking full sun or partial shade. If growing in a pot, the soil should be kept evenly moist, and I usually grow this grass in a self-watering container, using a soil mix of one-third each potting soil, composted manure, and sharp sand. Fertilize every month or so.

Palm grass loves a waterside site, but once established can be quite drought resistant. If planted out in the garden, remember the roots do not tolerate prolonged temperatures below 40° F, so in regions colder than Zone 9 dig up the plant and bring into a warmer place for the winter. This grass can be a pest in warm areas as it easily seeds about. Propagate by seed or division. Zones 9 to 11.

Sorghastrum nutans [*S. avenaceum, Chrysopogon nutans*], Indian grass or gold beard grass, is one of the big prairie grasses, named for the Native Americans. This is a beautiful grass, with roots so penetrating that plants easily survived flash fires that often swept the prairies years ago. It is a warm-season clumping grass with half-inch-wide leaves up to a foot long, branching off from the upright culms at a 45 degree angle. Usually plants are about three feet tall but they can reach five feet if the soil is moist and fertile. In late summer the showy yellowish-tan panicles appear, the spikelets bearing bright yellow anthers that turn golden-brown after the autumn frost (hence the common name of gold beard), when the foliage turns bright orange. The generic name is from *sorghum* and the Latin suffix, *astrum*, meaning "a poor imitation of," refers to the plant's resemblance to true sorghum. Provide a good, rich, moist soil in full sun to very light shade. Propagation is by seed and two seasons are needed (the first year is spent on root growth) for an established plant. Zones 5 to 9.

Sorghastrum nutans

Spartina pectinata [*Spartina michauxiana*], or cord grass, has additional common names that include bull grass, tall marsh grass, slough grass (*slough* is an old Anglo-Saxon word meaning "a wet or marshy place"), freshwater cord grass, and, my favorite, Upland Creek stuff. It only goes to show that when a plant becomes an integral part of a culture, it is known by many common names. Once a dominant grass of the tall grass prairies of the north central United States, cord grass was used by American pioneers to thatch roofs, protect haystacks from the weather, provide an inexpensive mulch, stuff archery targets, and control beach erosion. This grass is found from Maine to Oregon, then south to North Carolina, and west to Texas.

The variegated variety, 'Aureomarginata', or golden-edged prairie grass, is the type usually

Spartina pectinata

found on the market. A warm-season grass, it's one of the few that grows well with wet feet, and does best in full sun on moist soils—but it will tolerate average or even dry soil. For those gardening on the coasts, this grass will tolerate salt and brackish water. All cord grasses can be aggressive spreaders, so use some kind of barrier. In my garden, this grass is planted in a large, thick plastic tub buried beneath the soil surface. Propagate by seed or division. Zones 5 to 9.

Spodiopogon sibiricus, Siberian graybeard or frost grass, is one of a ten-species genus of grasses from temperate Asia and the Middle East. They tend to grow in forest glades and on steep hillsides. The generic name is from the Greek *spodios*, or "ashen," and *pogon*, for "beard," referring to the gray hairs on the flower spikes.

This is a warm-season grass somewhat like bamboo in appearance, with fuzzy bright green leaves about an inch wide and up to eight inches long. Like Indian grass, the leaves stick out from the culms at a 45 degree angle. As the season moves along, the leaves take on a reddish-purple tint. The flowers begin blooming in August and appear as an airy panicle with shiny purple spikelets, the panicles rising more than a foot above the foliage. Those small hairs on the blossoms will gleam in the sunlight of early morning or late afternoon. With the arrival of frost, the plants become a rich purple-brown. Provide a good, fertile, moist, and well-drained soil in full sun to partial shade. Zone 5 to cooler Zone 9.

Spodiopogon sibiricus

Sporobolus is a genus of some 100 species consisting of annual and perennial grasses that bear small spikelets in open or contracted panicles. The scientific name is from the Greek *spora*, or "seed," and *ballein*, "to throw," referring to the fact that in some species, there appear to be two seeds where there is really only one.

Sporobolus airoides, the alkali dropseed or alkali sacaton, is a graceful and beautiful grass native to much of the Southwest. The narrow leaves, up to three-eighths of an inch wide, are up to two feet long, forming dense clumps of gray-green leaves in mounds up to three feet tall and with the same width. The flowers appear from June through midsummer, consisting of delicate pink panicles best described as fuzzy clouds, which turn a golden tan with the advancing of autumn and shatter with the rains of November. The foliage turns a beautiful straw color for winter. Provide a moist, well-drained soil in full sun. This grass is tough and very tolerant, adapting to many conditions, including drought and (as its common name suggests) alkaline and salty conditions. Propagate by seed or division. Zones 7 to 9.

Sporobolus heterolepis, or prairie dropseed, named by our English cousins, is an elegant and refined North American prairie grass that belongs in every border that can support it. In its stunning catalogue, Chiltern Seeds describes it as a dense, flowing mound, fifteen inches tall, " . . . of the finest texture composed of the thinnest of thin, thread-like glossy green blades. In autumn, the clump turns a conspicuous deep orange before fading to a light copper for the winter. In late summer the plants bear, on very slender stalks high above the foliage, unbelievably delicate, graceful flower panicles, excellent for cutting. And a completely unexpected bonus: They are perfumed with a fragrance, delicate, sweet or

pungent; a blend of coriander and slightly burnt buttered popcorn! Delicious!"

This Texas native is a slow grower, a great ground cover, elegant when massed in the border and delightful in a good container, and attracts wildlife to the garden. While tolerating various growing conditions, it's best in well-drained soil in full sun. Propagate by seed or division, remembering that it takes two or three seasons to get a mature plant. Zones 4 to 9.

***Stenotaphrum secundatum* 'Variegatum'**, or variegated St. Augustine grass, spreads quickly by stolons and with great dispatch. The non-variegated species is often used as a lawn grass in the Deep South, where it responds quite well to

Sporobolus heterolepis

Stenotaphrum secundatum 'Variegatum'

mowing. The leaves of this cultivar are usually half an inch wide and up to four inches long, striped with creamy yellow-white stripes. It makes an excellent potted plant in the mountains of the Southeast or, in warmer areas, a useful ground cover. It is also very effective planted at the edge of a wall so the wandering stolons drip gracefully over the edge. Being a creeping grass, it will spread quickly and root along the stems. Insignificant flowers appear in the fall. Provide a moist, well-drained soil in full sun or light shade. Propagate by division or by stem cuttings.

Note: In the hot humid conditions of the Deep South, this grass can develop rust and invite chinch bug attacks. If that occurs, contact your county Extension agent. When variegated leaves revert to green, remove them immediately. Zone 10 (Zone 9 with protection).

***

Stipa represents the needle grasses or feather grasses, their common name referring to the long and often twisted awns that project from the spikelets. Some of these grasses are dangerous because of the sharp points on the seeds that enable them to penetrate fur and skin, and are

Stipa capillata

carried off for eventual germination. And sleepy grass (*Stipa robusta*) is said to act as a stultifying drug on animals that graze upon it. The genus is from the Greek *stupe*, or "tow" (short, coarse fibers of flax or hemp used for making yarn), referring to those feathery awns found in many of the species.

A wild stipa of the prairies is called porcupine grass (*Stipa spartea*), and it uses its twisted awn to guarantee future seed germination. When the floret falls from the flower stem, it sticks the pointed end into the earth where barbed hairs prevent it from pulling out. The awn then coils and uncoils with changes in humidity, and when it luckily lodges itself beside a stray bit of plant debris or a small stone that provides support, the seed proceeds to drill itself into the soil, where it germinates.

Stipa capillata, or feather grass, is a clumper famous for the upright silky panicles that glisten in every shaft of sunlight. The narrow, fourth-inch leaves grow about two feet long and are topped with flowers towering two feet above the plants. Provide a good, well-drained soil in full sun and, remember, the smaller forms look great in the rock garden. Propagate by seed, as dividing doesn't always succeed. Zone 6 to cooler Zone 9.

Stipa gigantea, or giant feather grass, sometimes called golden oats, is a monumental grass from Spain and Portugal that beckons to every adventurous gardener. The first time I saw this beauty was on a garden tour to the gardens of southern England, where Christopher Lloyd featured it as a specimen plant. A Spanish native, the seven-foot stalks of this grass resemble a graceful bamboo blooming with ten-inch, airy panicles of oat-like flowers that open as a greenish-purple but mature to a pale, metallic gold. The gray-green leaves make a demure clump of two-foot

Stipa gigantea

leaves, with the flowering panicles shooting out like fireworks. This clumping, evergreen, cool-season beauty belongs in your backyard but only if your garden is warm enough and the soil is well drained—damp, freezing winter soil will lead to defeat. Propagate by seed, remembering that germination is slow. Zones 7 to 9.

Stipa ichu, the Peruvian feather grass, is a clumping evergreen grass with very thin bright green leaves that make an elegant mound about three feet high and just as wide. Very showy flowers appear in the spring, sporting those silky awns common to the genus. They begin as silver and mature to a golden yellow. A native of the Andean mountains of Peru and Chile, these grasses need a fertile and well-drained soil in full sun. They are beautiful when massed in the

border or grown as a specimen plant in an elegant container. They are very heat resistant, and while scree soil is the key, amazingly they will adapt even to clay—but good drainage is absolutely necessary; these grasses need great drainage to survive. They will tolerate some shade, but not too much. Propagate by seed. Zone 8 to cooler Zone 10.

Stipa pennata, or European feather grass, gets its common name from the very long and feathery awns, up to twelve inches long, that twist about in the wind. Originally from central and southern Europe, the narrow gray-green leaves grow in neat mounds with flowering stems up to thirty inches, topped by all those awns following the direction of the prevailing winds. Absolutely beautiful. Zones 5 to 8.

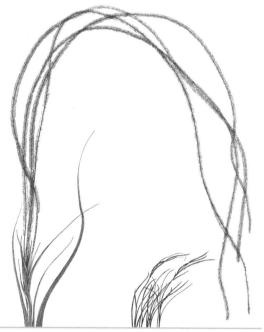

Stipa pennata

Stipa ramosissima [*Austrostipa ramosissima*], or pillar-of-smoke grass, is a cool-season evergreen grass with stunning flowers. These blossoms actually bloom along the stems, suggesting a pillar of smoke. The bright green leaves are up to a fourth of an inch wide and about ten inches long, wrapping themselves around stout culms, each about the thickness of a pencil and up to five feet long, making the entire clump up to seven feet in height. The flowers begin to appear in early spring and continue the floral advance into summer. They emerge as a silky bronze, maturing to a cream color, finally fading to gray. Plants remain evergreen in mild climates. This is a great grass when massed in the back of the border (or for a change, make it the one high point at the front of the border) or grown in an elegant pot set out in the garden. Both heat and drought tolerant, it will probably be a star of Southern gardens. Propagate by seed because division can sometimes be chancy. Zones 8 to 9.

Stipa tenuissima

Stipa tenuissima [*Nassella tenuissima*], or, as it's known in the trade, Mexican feather grass, is another American native that has hit the big time. A. S. Hitchcock described it in the 1950 edition of the *Manual of the Grasses of the United States* as being at home in the open dry woods and rocky slopes of Texas and New Mexico. The genus name *Stipa* is from the Greek *stupe*, or "tow," alluding to the feathery awns. There has recently been a name change and now some botanists have assigned this grass to the genus *Nassella* (from the Latin *nassa*, a narrow-necked basket for catching fish, referring to the shape of the florets in some species), but until the name goes up in lights, I'll stick to *Stipa*.

This is an extremely fine-textured grass, much like a diminutive or short-necked relative of the Addam's Family Cousin Itt, but with far more charm and grace. It grows in wispy tufts to about two feet high with a two-foot width, consisting of bright green thread-like leaves that in midsummer are topped by soft, plume-like flower spikes, which hunker down into the foliage. As fall approaches, the leaves turn a light straw color and remain viable clumps well into the winter, instead of falling to pieces like many grasses left to wind and rain. Provide full sun or light shade and, remember that if space is limited, these grasses are elegant in fancy pots. Plants are very drought resistant and have few demands outside a well-drained but slightly moist soil. These plants self-seed and can become weedy invaders. Zones 6 to 9.

Uniola paniculata, sea oats or spike grass, is a rhizomatous grass that grows on and protects coastal sand dunes from Virginia down to eastern Mexico. It's probably most familiar to beach combers and vacation visitors. It's an ideal grass for stabilizing dunes and halting erosion and does well, in general, for coastal

Uniola paniculata

gardening—and is attractive enough to merit attention. It is, however, a protected plant, so prospective gardeners should contact their local Extension agents to find legitimate sources for plants. Zones 7 to 10.

Vetiveria zizanoides, or, as it's more popularly known, khus-khus, is an Asian grass native to the Old World tropics where it has enjoyed a reputation for being both an exotic perfume and an ingredient in island cooking. It is also known as vetiver grass because of its ability to fix other aromas so their fragrance lingers on human skin, and the oil distilled from the roots has a great value in making perfumes. In India, khus-khus has long been an ingredient of perfumes and dampened khus-khus mats were used as fans to move and perfume the air.

While generally benign, khus-khus has been involved in political problems because, in India and many Arab countries, the grass is also known as *khas-khas*, this second popular name also being the term used for ripe seeds of the opium poppy (*Papaver somniferum*)—and having those on your person can mean legal problems beyond belief.

On a friendlier note, if you have khus-khus, cut a few leaves in small pieces and soak them in distilled or rain water for three days or more, and you'll have a very fragrant toilet water for personal use.

On a more productive front, there is a worldwide organization that promotes the use of khus-khus in fighting erosion—the roots are actually called "soil nails." Their Web site is www.vetiver.org, a great place to browse on a rainy afternoon.

The generic name refers to *vettiver*, an old native Tamil name for a coarse grass, while *zizanoides* hearkens back to the genus *Zizania*, from *zizanion*, an old Greek name for a weed found growing in grain.

I first met this grass at the Missouri Botanical Garden in St. Louis. On the brick pavement in one of the herb gardens were two big clay containers, each with the six-foot, straight shafts of the grass pointing skyward, the individual blades bent over about three inches from the tips, almost as though the folds had been made by human hands. The individual blades are a light green but as fall approaches, they are colored with bronzy-

Vetiveria zizanoides

purple tints. When in bloom the plants produce large erect panicles with slender whorled branches, but unless you live in the Deep South, plants in pots rarely flower.

Propagation is by division as there are two forms of this grass, one sterile and one not. Usually nurseries market the sterile form. Zones 9 and 10.

I grant you that this grass will not overwinter in our mountain gardens, but it's a boon to gardeners in warmer climes. If taken indoors before the frosts of fall, plants easily winter over in a sunroom, greenhouse, or the garage, as long as temperatures stay about 45° F and the soil is kept reasonably dry.

Zeugites americana var. *mexicana*

Zeugites americana var. mexicana, is a grass that I acquired from one of the more adventurous seed companies, Trans-Pacific

Zeugites americana var. *mexicana*

Nursery. It was described in the catalog as a grass that appeared to be a species of bamboo, but flowered so frequently, without dying, that they were suspicious. It turns out to be a grass that may reach a height of two feet on very thin, weeping or trailing stems. The leaves are small, about a half-inch long and broadly ovate, with some leaves variegated. Plants do well at the edge of a pond or in a container. Zones 9 and 10. The genus refers to the Greek word *zeugitès*, meaning an owner of a span of oxen or a citizen owning enough to serve in political office. The connection escapes me. Propagation is by division.

Zizania latifolia, or Manchurian wild rice, is the perennial form of wild rice and hails from the Far East, including China, Korea, and eastern Siberia. Leaves are a little over an inch wide and green in the summer. But this species is particularly beautiful in the fall when the rustling foliage turns a beautiful yellow. The plants need shallow water and can reach a height of four to six feet. The flowers appear in dense, upright panicles, and begin blooming around mid-August. The lower flowers are male, opening first and resembling old lacework. The upper flowers on the stem are female and eventually form the seeds. The generic name is from an old Greek word for a weed found growing in fields of grain. Propagate by seed and division in spring. Zones 7 to 9.

Note: **Zizania texana**, or Texas wild rice, is a rare and endangered species of aquatic rice that grows in the headwaters of the San Marcos River, well within the city limits of the city of San Marcos. It is only found in this location and is now a protected species. There should be a movement to distribute seeds to caring gardeners in an effort to save this valuable resource.

THE SEDGES, THE RUSHES, THE HORSETAILS, AND THE RESTIOS

For two great plant families representing many species that are perfect for the garden and easily mistaken for ornamental grasses, look to the Cyperaceae, or the sedges, and the Juncaceae, or the rushes.

The sedges consist of some eighty genera, with about 3,000 species, of worldwide distribution, often growing in wet or damp places, usually aquatic or semi-aquatic, and sometimes terrestrial. The rushes are represented by eight genera with some 300 species and consist of the true aquatic plants that grow in wet places or directly in water, and the terrestrial woodrushes that prefer drier locations, often in shaded woodlands.

Some species of the Cyperaceae and the Juncaceae are very easy to confuse with the true grasses, but those who have taken botany may remember this old poem:

> Sedges have edges,
> Rushes are round,
> And grasses are hollow
> Like a hole in the ground.

There are other ways to spot the difference between a grass and a sedge. Sedge culms lack nodes, are usually solid (filled with pith), and have three ranks of leaves. Also, using a hand lens, you will find that grass flowers have six stamens, while sedges have only one to three.

The Sedges

Of all the recognized species, only a few members of the sedge family are cultivated as ornamentals (and a few as a source of food). These true sedges occur from the tropics to the arctic, growing well in mud, water, and damp soils in general, preferring spots in full sun or light shade.

For economic value, on a scale of one to ten, most people would probably give them a generous minus-fifty, but they truly are valuable members of the plant world. Sedges grow and revel in swamps, marshes, ditches—just drive backwoods roads in summer to see the magnificent sedges in a backwater ditch by the roadside. There they form an intermediate step between seemingly useless mud (at least to mankind) and valuable dry land by spreading their rhizomes and acting as a landfill that eventually allows other vegetation to grow.

Because sedge stems are very dry and most lack

Juncus effusus 'Unicorn'

117

Carex albula 'Frosted Curls'

starches and sugars, they are of little use as animal food. However, the sea club rush (*Scirpus maritimus*), a common species of seacoast salt marshes (and not a true rush), has sweet rootstocks and is used as pig food in Sweden. The common bulrush (*Scirpus lacustris*) is often used in the manufacture of rush-bottomed chairs (this plant is not a true rush either). The earth almond or Zulu nut (*Cyperus esculentus* var. *sativus*) produces an edible tuber that is roasted for food and ground up as flour (although there is a continual argument over its use as a food and its potential threat as a noxious weed).

Sedges grow in a variety of soil types but most species do best in acidic or slightly acidic conditions, with their ultimate height and hardiness determining their use in the landscape. *Carex nigra* grows about eight inches high, *Carex morrowii* usually stays about two feet high, and *Carex pendula* makes a mound of leaves from two to three feet high (with blooming stems extending four feet).

Leaf color varies from reddish-brown to copper-red, from a glaucous powdery blue to a rich chartreuse green, from yellow to a deep green to great variegations, while the seedpods of many species are enough reason to grow the plant.

Finally, some sedges produce bisexual flower spikes, while in other species male and female spikes are borne separately. Many of the sedges have very attractive and often interesting seedheads. The great weeping sedge (*Carex pendula*), is well worth having despite its tendency to seed about, not only for the mound of foliage, but for the wand-like stems hung with catkin-like flower spikes. *Carex baccans* sports bright red seeds and *Carex grayi* is known in England as the mace sedge because of its spiky, inflated, pale-green seedheads, which resemble the medieval weapon of that name.

Sedges are easy to care for once their water demands are met. Like ornamental grasses, deciduous species can be cut back in early spring before the new growth appears, and the evergreen types will benefit if the gardener removes dead or damaged leaves.

The sedges listed here belong to the genus *Carex*, the genus *Cymophyllus*, the genus *Cyperus*, the genus *Eleocharis*, the genus *Scirpus*, and a few lesser-known members of this family.

The Carexes

The following are among the most attractive species and cultivars belonging to the *Carex* genus on the nursery market today. Many come

Carex plantaginea

Carex grayi and *Carex pendula*

Carex albula

from Japan, many from New Zealand, a few from Europe and England, plus some great plants that are native Americans and especially productive in the Southeast. *Carex* is the Latin name for sedge. Another source claims that *Carex* is from the Greek *keiro*, "to cut," referring to the minutely toothed leaf margins often capable of cutting a finger or a hand. The word "sedge" is from the Anglo-Saxon *secg*, meaning a small sword or dagger, referring to the narrow, pointed leaves of these plants.

This is a quickly changing group of plants and every year new carex introductions show up at the various nurseries. There is no way of keeping up with sedge progress, so I apologize in advance that I have included only those selections that I found available up to the midsummer of 2003.

Carex albula [*Carex comans*] is known as the New Zealand hair sedge but sometimes as the green wig. A fine-textured, evergreen sedge, it forms dense tufts of very thin, light green leaves greatly resembling a head of hair in need of a trim. *Comans* is from the Latin word for hairy. These hair-like leaves are usually about a foot long but well-grown plants can reach a length of at least four feet. Flowering is insignificant, but save the small pods for the seeds. In nature these plants do best along the edge of a stream but need a well-drained soil. And, paradoxically, they are somewhat drought tolerant. The only problem with this plant is that like many New Zealand plants brought to this country, they are sometimes

Carex albula 'Variegata'

short lived. But *Carex albula* grows easily from seed. Unlike most sedges, these plants like a neutral to a slightly alkaline soil. Zones 7 to 9.

There are many cultivars, including 'Bronze', popular for the color of the foliage; 'Frosted Curls', with leaves that curl like pigtails at the edges, with the tips a frosty-white in color; and 'Variegata,' the miniature variegated sedge—in March 2003, two of these charmers are blooming in my garden just above a stone wall. These are small, clumping plants with silvery-white variegations, and grow about six inches high.

Carex baccans

Carex baccans, the crimson seed sedge, is originally from India and South Asia. Plants grow from two to four feet high, their leaves long and curving. The fruit is berry-like (botanically known as a perigynia-covered achene), coral-red to shining purple when ripe and, although small,

a hefty bunch of these very small fruits can bend the stalks with their weight. In fact, the species name of *baccans* means "with berries." This is a great accent plant for full sun to partial shade and the seed stalks are excellent in arrangements. Provide a good, moist soil. Well-grown plants will survive a few degrees of freezing but if frost is a problem, it's best to bring them indoors as greenhouse plants. They are easily grown from seed. Zones 8 to 9.

Carex buchananii

Carex buchananii, the leather leaf sedge, has probably been seen by more people than any other sedge. Named for John Buchanan (1819–1898), a student of New Zealand flora, this great sedge appears in one of the scenes from the first *Lord of the Rings* movie saga, where our heroes wend their way across a grassy plain filmed in New Zealand. They are surrounded by dense and erect tussocks, up to two and a half feet high, of gracefully bending leaves with a very fine texture, and a color variously described as reddish green or coppery brown. The plants are most conspicuous when planted in large dark-colored pots or grown in large clumps in the border or rock garden, providing great fall and winter color. Propagate by seed or by division, providing a bit of shade in moist, but well-drained, soil. They can be grown indoors in a humid greenhouse. Unless conditions are perfect, this sedge is not long lived, usually lasting up to three years in the garden. Zones 7 to 9.

Carex caryophyllea 'Beatlemania' is a new cultivar on the hort-rock scene, in common parlance called the striped mop-top sedge and dedicated to the haircuts that the Beatles sported in the 1960s. Some say it's a variegated form of the selection called 'The Beatles', and according to Tony Avent of Plant Delights Nursery, was a selection made by Alan Tower of Spokane, Washington. This clumping sedge is about a foot wide and bears very dark green leaves bordered with gold. While noted as slow growing, in the best soils it can eventually make a dense ground cover. Zones 5 to 7.

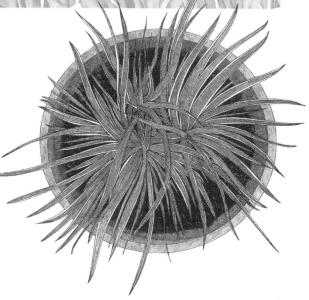

Carex conica

Carex caryophyllea 'Beatlemania'

Carex conica is a truly beautiful little sedge from Japan that is often grown as a houseplant. The narrow leaves range from an eighth to three-eighths of an inch in width, are deep green, and curve slightly as they grow, eventually reaching a six-inch length. As the plant ages, it slowly becomes a clump.

I featured the variegated form in my 1973 book on grasses, calling it the miniature variegated sedge, the common name in use at the time. I'm reminded of Shakespeare's line about roses by any other name still being sweet, and with the increasing number of names given to this little plant, assume this is an honor. Today, look for that plant as 'Snowline', 'Marginata', 'Variegata', and 'Hime Kansuge' (or sometimes as 'Himekansuge'). In this form the deep green, curved leaves are edged with white, and that border of white is applied with extreme precision.

On a sunny day in early April, I took a few moments to go out to the back stone wall in our lake garden where I have five little carexes of this variety—in bloom, bearing upright stems tipped with elongated brownish matchheads and seeming to be pleasantly ensconced. Good light, sun in the mountains and partial shade everywhere else, coupled with moist soil, are the requirements. A lack of humidity and a too warm environment will cause the leaves to turn brown. Evergreen. Zone 5 to 9.

Carex dipsacea is an attractive New Zealand sedge that, according to catalogs, grows on the mountainsides of the Lewis Pass. Chiltern Seeds remarks its suitability for the smaller garden because the plant forms small to medium dense clumps of very narrow, erect, green leaves that boast orange highlights in the spring. The clumps eventually reach a height of twenty-some inches. In autumn, stems bearing black seedheads appear, the seed being bristly or resembling a teasel head, as Jacob Berggren (1790–1868), the botanist who named the plant thought. Hence the species name of *dipsacea* or "teasel-like." This sedge prefers sun to partial shade. Zone 6 to 9.

Carex dolichostachya 'Kaga Nishiki'

Carex dolichostachya [*Carex foliosissima*] is known as *Miyama-kan-suge* in Japan where it grows in the woods along mountains around Hokkaido, Honshu, and Kyushu. The very attractive cultivar 'Kaga Nishiki' is often sold in the trade as *Carex* 'Gold Fountains'. It's a selection of the form *glaberrima*, and easily grown in medium to wet soils, with partial shade to almost full shade in the Deep South—remembering that these plants must never be allowed to dry out. The individual clumps spread up to twenty inches wide and about fourteen inches high. This sedge bears fine-textured, narrow, bright green leaves about three-sixteenths of an inch wide, edged with

yellow, arching up and out like a small fountain. In a moderate winter climate the leaves are evergreen but should be sheared off in late winter to make room for new growth. Zones 6 to 9.

Carex elata

Carex elata [sometimes called *Carex flava* and *C. stricta*] is in itself not a very decorative sedge. But the cultivar 'Bowles Golden', when discovered in the first half of the last century growing on the Norfolk Broads in England by plantsman E. A. Bowles, was something else again. Bowles first grew it in his "Lunatic Asylum," a special garden he devoted to unusual plants. But when the colorful aspects of this plant were finally brought to terms with the rest of the garden, 'Bowles Golden' became a hit. The bright golden-yellow leaves are irregularly striped with bright green and reach a height of over two feet. These sedges are great for containers, planted in clumps, or massed in the border (a bit of black plastic placed under the roots at planting time can hold the needed moisture), or arranged in a natural fashion by a pond or stream. Zones 6 to 8.

***Carex elegantissima* 'Variegata'** is the popular cultivar of the species and the only variety I've ever found offered in the nursery trade. It would seem that the species must be attractive, although I have not found a picture—but the cultivar is very beautiful in its own right. It's a fine-textured plant, not hair-like but close to it, with two-foot evergreen leaves, each about an eighth of an inch wide, and graced with a golden edge. Not-too-important flowers on one-foot stems appear in the summer. These plants are best in a semi-shaded area as the leaves can burn under a hot Southern sun. They require moist, well-drained, and fertile soil and resent a lack of water. Propagation is by division. Zones 8 to 9.

Carex firma grows in the mountains of central Europe and is, so far, the smallest sedge in existence. Unless sited in a perfect spot, its hard and narrowly triangular leaves rarely exceed one inch long, their dark green color like a flash of brilliance when surrounded by stony scree. The leaves arise from a rosette that clings close to the ground. The species name means "firm," "dense," and "not hollow"—and they are just that. These sedges do beautifully in tiny pots or carefully planted in a lime-rich soil with perfect drainage. In the Edinburgh Botanic Garden I saw them carefully set between flat stones where any true description of them contains the word "cute." Zones 6 to 9.

***Carex firma* 'Variegata'** has each leaf carefully edged with a band of creamy yellow and is even more desirable than the species. Zones 6 to 9.

Carex flaccosperma, the blue wood sedge, is a great native ground cover native from southern Virginia down to Florida and then west to Texas, where its natural habitats are wet woods and swamps. This sedge is a slow creeper, mixing well with ferns and native wildflowers in a wooded garden. The clumps are about ten inches tall with bluish, quilted, half-inch wide leaves.

Rob Gardner, a curator at The North Carolina Botanical Garden in Chapel Hill, wrote: "This attractive evergreen southeastern native is very suitable for woodland conditions, as its color and vigor seem to suffer when planted in full sun."

Gardner likes to see this plant set out at the edge of a stream or pool, next to rocks, or even beside a ditch. He also notes that it has a small quirk that when in the flowering and fruiting phase, the plants have a tendency to lean on and co-mingle with their neighbors in "unexpected and charming ways." Prefers light shade and damp soil. Zones 5 to 8.

Carex flagellifera, or the weeping brown New Zealand sedge, got its species name from its long thin whip-like fruits. On its home turf it lives in damp soil along the edges of forest thickets. The plants form three-foot-tall, dense tussocks of shiny bronze leaves usually about two feet in length, with leaves arching to the ground, with whip-like tips. The seedheads appear on tall three- to four-foot stems and are best cut off soon after flowering, as they eventually fall back upon the plants and look very untidy. Provide a moist, well-drained soil with a bit of afternoon shade, especially in the Deep South. After a few years of growth these plants begin to look wildly unkempt, so cut them back to six inches above the central crown and growth will begin again. Propagation is by division or by seed. Zones 7 to 9.

Carex glauca [*Carex flacca*], or the blue sedge, grows as an evergreen creeper bearing slightly pleated leaves of blue, and nondescript blue-stemmed flowers in early summer. *Glauca* is from the Latin word for blue-green. Plant height can be up to a foot but usually stays in the six-inch range. It's an excellent (albeit slow) ground cover originally from Europe, where it grows in open fields and the edges of woodlands. If the plant ranges into an area where it's unwelcome, the invaders are easily pulled up and given to friends. Blue sedge is also a fine choice for edging a pathway or border. Here in our Asheville garden, it survives above ground most winters but has been known to suffer some leaf-burning from frost. Cut back browned foliage to a few inches in length. Provide a moist, fertile soil, with full sun at the northern range of the Southeast but partial shade where the sun is really hot. But like many plants that dote on moisture, blue sedge will adapt to dryer areas. The glaucous color makes it a good plant for naturalizing and as a lawn substitute in lightly shaded areas. Propagate by seed or by division. Zones 5 to 9.

Carex grayi, or Gray's sedge, produces a handsome clump of light green leaves with a

Carex grayi

papery texture that stays green well into the fall. The species was named in honor of America's great botanist, Asa Gray. Clumps can reach a height of three feet but usually measure in at two to two and a half. The grass-like leaves are up to a half-inch wide. While adaptable to most soils and locations, this sedge does appreciate moist soil and good sun, with only a bit of dappled shade. The flowers of midsummer give rise to a fruiting body that looks for all the world like a miniature model of the glass and wrought-iron hanging lights found in the hallways of Spanish stucco houses in the 1920s. These fruits are attractive in both fresh and dried arrangements and remain on the plant in winter. When out in the wild, look for plants along streams and brooks flowing through open woods. Propagation is through division or seed. Zones 6 to 8.

Carex morrowii [*Carex japonica*] was, before the many cultivars appeared, commonly known as Morrow's sedge and recognized or grown by only a few gardeners and horticulturists. Then 'Variegata', the most common cultivar, hit the nursery trade, and history and fashion together made their mark. Rarely grown as the species, Morrow's sedge is the broadest-leaved of the clump-growing sedges, and bears tough, glossy leaves up to three-eighths of an inch wide and from twelve to sixteen inches long, arching over at the tips in typical fountain form. Provide moist, well-drained soil in light shade or partial shade. These sedges resent drying out and if the sun is too hot, their leaves will burn. Propagate by seeds in some cultivars and by division. All Morrow's sedges resent hot, humid weather and wet conditions. Zones 6 to 9; in Zones 9 and 10 use as a winter annual.

In the garden these sedges are very valuable as edging in borders, bunched as specimens, or just planted in large masses. As a pot plant, Japanese sedges are excellent when grown in a potting mixture of peat moss, potting soil, and sharp sand—one-third each. Make sure the plants receive adequate light, and generally they will bloom in early spring. The flowers are not resplendent, as they resemble crushed camel's-hair brushes that have been dipped in yellow powder, but they are a welcome sight in late winter.

Carex morrowii 'Fisher's Form' grows to an eighteen-inch height and bears leaves edged in white. Partial shade is recommended. Zones 6 to 9.

Carex morrowii 'Goldband' or the golden variegated Japanese sedge, bears shiny green leaves carefully edged with golden yellow bands. The half-inch leaves artfully droop to the ground. This sedge requires well-drained and

Carex morrowii 'Ice Dance'

fertile soil with a constant supply of moisture. Do not let the plant dry out and keep protected from the hot noon sun. Zones 7 to 9.

Carex morrowii 'Ice Dance' is an improved form of 'Variegata' with broader leaves sporting ivory edges. This great new evergreen ground cover tolerates light and shade. Cut the leaves to the ground in late winter. Considered aggressive by some growers, it's not invasive, but will grow up to two feet in height and will spread, making a two- to three-foot clump. Zones 5 to 9.

Carex morrowii 'Silver Sceptre' curves to the ground in graceful bends with foot-long leaves, a fourth-inch wide, edged with ivory. Provide plenty of shade. Zones 5 to 9.

Carex morrowii 'Silver Sceptre'

Carex morrowii 'Silk Tassel'

Carex morrowii var. temnolepsis 'Silk Tassel' [*Carex temnolepis*], called *Hosoba kan suge* in Japan, is another one of those anthropomorphic carexes, looking like tiny green Pekinese pets running in place. The plants are mounds of dark green, stiff thread-like leaves with a definite silver midrib, growing about a foot high with the leaves barely an eighth of an inch wide. On my two plants I just cut back some of the browned foliage from last year, and ran my fingers through the leaves, like running fingers through hair. They must have moisture, partial shade, and, in the Deep South, protection from the sun. Zones 5 to 8.

Carex morrowii 'Variegata', or the silver variegated Japanese sedge, bears the typical foliage of the species, but in this form has faint silver margins on the leaves that echo the other incredibly thin but purposeful white lines. This sedge also needs a moist, rich soil in partial shade, and must have full shade in hot locations. Zones 5 to 9.

Carex muskingumensis, the palm sedge, gets its name from the plant's resemblance to miniature palm trees—curious when you realize these carexes are American natives from the low woods and wet meadows of Michigan, Ohio, and Kentucky, then west to Kansas and Oklahoma. The species name is in honor of Ohio's Muskingum River.

Carex muskingumensis

They are easily grown in good moist soil (although they will adapt to an average soil), and in partial shade as you journey down into the South. They do very well in shallow water (three to four inches), but if moved to a dryer spot must never be allowed to dry out. Cut them to the ground over winter.

Plants grow about twenty inches tall with eight-inch, grass-like, light green leaves that turn yellow with frost. Palm sedges spread by their rhizomes and make excellent ground covers. Propagate by seed or by division. Zones 5 to 9.

Carex muskingumensis 'Little Midge'

was an introduction from Norm Hooven of Limerock Ornamental Grasses in Pennsylvania, and is so named because it's a diminutive cultivar of the species, reaching a height of about ten inches, with palm-like bright green leaves. Zones 5 to 9.

Carex muskingumensis 'Oehme' was

introduced in 1994 by Tony Avent and is a sport originally found in Wolfgang Oehme's garden (of Oehme and Van Sweden, the famous landscape designers that have used ornamental grasses with such great effect). The leaves of this cultivar have a clear yellow border with the stripes appearing soon after the leaves unfold.

Carex muskingumensis 'Oehme'

Carex muskingumensis 'Wachtposten'

(meaning "sentry tower") is a cultivar that reaches a height between two and three feet, the light green leaves radiating from the stems like fans. Zones 5 to 9.

Carex nigra, the black-blooming sedge grass, is a native of Eurasia. Because of its blue-gray foliage with a powdery underside, it's often confused with *C. glauca*. These plants prefer wet soils, have leaves about a fourth-inch wide, and range in height from six to nine inches tall with a one- to three-foot spread. Flowers appear in early spring and bear almost black scales, blooming just above the leaves. This sedge is good in rock gardens and planted in masses, and will survive when planted in shallow water (three to four inches deep). A spreader but not strong enough to be labeled invasive. Provide partial shade. Propagate by seed or division. Zones 4 to 8.

Carex nigra 'Variegata' is a shorter

plant never topping nine inches with a twelve-inch spread. The variegation produces light green, grassy leaves edged with yellow instead of blue-gray foliage. Black flowers appear in early spring. It grows in shade but can tolerate a goodly amount of sun if kept constantly moist and never allowed to dry out. Like the species, this cultivar will adapt to a water depth of three to four inches. Evergreen in mild climates, the foliage usually disappears over winter in our Asheville garden. Propagate by division. Zones 5 to 8.

Carex nudata, or the California black-flowering sedge, isn't always easy to find but is well worth the effort. It's a clumping sedge with a deciduous habit, having gray-green leaves, a bit over two feet long and about a fourth of an inch wide. The leaves turn orange when touched by frost, then a light brown when winter arrives. Unlike *Carex nigra*, the flowers of this species are very showy, with similar black scales, but with flowering stems rising above the drooping foliage to great effect. Provide full sun to partial shade but protect from a burning southern sun. This sedge loves a spot at the edge of a water feature or shallow water three to four inches deep. Like many sedges, this selection will grow well in pots. Propagate by seed or division. Zones 7 to 9.

Carex ornithipoda 'Variegata', or the variegated bird's foot sedge, is a native of Great Britain where it's a very localized plant, chiefly growing in limestone turf in the northern half of England. Over there it's called the small-fingered sedge, and it's really a toss-up as to which common name is the best. Both refer to the flower habit, the blooms resembling either a bird's foot or a hand. The small clumps reach six inches in height with spreading flower spikes. The cultivar is so named for the white, longitudinally variegated leaves. Unless you live in the mountains of North Carolina, South Carolina, or Georgia, you had best cultivate this treasure in a dish garden, where it will immediately charm all your garden friends. In the mountains, provide calcareous, well-drained, humus-rich soil. Zones 7 to 9, but not for the hotter areas of Zone 9.

Carex oshimensis 'Evergold'

Carex oshimensis 'Evergold' [*Carex morrowii* 'Evergold' and *C. hachijoensis* 'Evergold'] has, at last, finally arrived at its nomenclatural home. One of the oldest cultivars to be grown in American and European gardens, in Japan the species is known as *Oshima-kan-suge* and is found in dry woods and rocky slopes. This is a tough sedge, forming clumps of bright creamy-yellow leaves, with the color applied down the leaf center. These leaves are a little over a fourth-inch in width, reaching a sixteen-inch height but arching over to create a plant about ten inches high and fifteen inches across. This sedge grows best in well drained but moist soil, resents drying out, and in the southern sun needs partial shade, especially in the afternoon. Rumor has it that plants sometimes revert to the species type and lose their variegations. If that happens in your garden, you can cut back the offending leaves, but the green form is also very attractive. Propagate by division in the spring. Zones 7 to 9.

Carex oshimensis 'Variegata' is very close to *C. morrowii* 'Variegata' as described in a previous entry. In this form the leaves have a pale central stripe edged with green, while in the *C. morrowii* cultivar, the variegation is reversed, with leaves having pale margins and green centers.

Carex pansa [*Carex praegracilis*] is a little sedge with big ambitions. The popular scientific name is in bold type (and for the life of me I cannot find the derivation of the species name). In square brackets is the scientific name that some botanists think is correct (in this case, the species name refers to the plants at first being thin and slender until they make little tufts and spread about).

According to *The New Britton and Brown Illustrated Flora of the Northeastern United States and Adjacent Canada*, *C. praegracilis* is a sedge that lives on moist soils, chiefly on the prairies and extends from Iowa to Oklahoma, then up to the Yukon, and west to California. John Greenlee in his excellent book, *The Encyclopedia of Ornamental Grasses*, describes it as a plant of California to Washington, growing on sand dunes and coastal plains, and calls it the California meadow sedge. Such is the stuff of sorting out specimens and scientific names.

That said, C. *pansa* is a small creeping dune plant that when settling in makes little colonial tufts. It is not an aggressive plant and can be overwhelmed by many of the invasive and alien grasses such as the brome grasses from Eurasia. Greenlee suggests that the plant makes a fine lawn substitute or an unmowed meadow. With plant height about four inches, the rich green leaves—up to an eighth of an inch wide and eight inches long—make dense colonies of their decorative ribbon-ends growth patterns.

Mr. Greenlee also points out that this sedge is basically untested for the hotter parts of the South and perhaps with those conditions C. *pensylvanica* would be a better choice. Provide moist, well-drained soil in full sun or partial shade, and it's great for beach plantings. Without plenty of water it goes dormant during extremely hot weather. Zones 8 to 9.

Carex pendula [*Carex capillaris*], the great weeping sedge or, as I prefer to call it, the great pendulous wood sedge, is a close relative to the lesser pendulous wood sedge (*Carex sylvatica*) and the lesser marsh sedge (*Carex acutiformis*), and one of the tallest of these grass-like plants. A well-grown specimen becomes a fountain of light green leaves, usually over four feet in height. The spikelets consist of three- to five-inch catkin-like flowers, formed on very thin stems that are often up to six feet long, persisting well into winter. These stems resemble wands that arch out in all

Carex pendula

directions. When a light summer breeze rustles the leaves, it sounds like unwrapping the tissue paper of a Christmas present. If allowed to grow undisturbed, these plants make a sizeable statement, and when planted next to water, you get the double beauty of the plant's reflections. Originally imported into England in 1600, this sedge is easily grown from seed from mail-order sources if plants are unavailable. Cut back the old leaves in early spring before the new growth appears.

Provide a good moist soil, in full sun in our northern range and partial shade in the Deep South, remembering that this sedge can get very large and once established is quite difficult to move. Zones 6 to 9.

Carex pendula 'Moonraker' is a new cultivar that is, so far, only available in England. But it's such a beautiful plant I must mention it here so that over the next few seasons, gardeners can be on the lookout for this stunner. This lovely variegated plant bears pale yellow leaves that gradually turn to green as they age. It also has a perfect cultivar name. Zones 6 to 9.

Carex pensylvanica, the yellow sedge, also known as the Pennsylvania sedge, Penn sedge, and early sedge, is a native plant that grows low to the ground and makes a beautiful mat of attractive medium green foliage about six to eight inches high. Recently this sedge has proven valuable as a low-maintenance alternative to the typical "English-style" lawn, especially around dry and shady sites. The Pennsylvania sedge enjoys a wide range and is found from Nova Scotia to South Carolina then west to North Dakota, Iowa, and Tennessee, with a variety (C. *pensylvanica* var. *pacificum*) spreading around Puget Sound in Washington. The narrow leaves are from four to eighteen inches long and about the same height as the stems. These sedges are noted for providing resources for migratory waterfowl, ducks finding the leaves perfect for both cover and nesting material. Here in Asheville, along the city part of Town Mountain Road, this sedge associates with alumroot (*Heuchera* spp.) and the beautiful wildflower Bowman's root (*Gillenia trifoliata*). Zones 4 to 8.

Carex petrei, the dark brown sedge, or Petrei's sedge, is another native of New Zealand, described as having bronze, thread-like leaves that grow in a twisted manner, curling at their tips, and looking for all the world like brown steel-wool. They require constant moisture and must have great drainage. If these conditions are within your grasp, this is a great plant for rock gardens or growing in a pot. Like many of the plants imported from New Zealand, they often have a short life span, especially in hot climates—no matter how you bend to the wishes of some species, to them there's no place like home. But with the charms they offer, they're worth every effort. In Zone 9, provide a bit of afternoon shade. Propagate by seed or division. Zones 7 to 9.

Carex phyllocephala 'Sparkler'

Carex phyllocephala 'Sparkler' is known in Japan as *Tenjiku-suge*, a common name that some errant nursery copyeditors have turned into the Tenjiku sedge. The species name translates as "having leafy heads." This is one beautiful plant: It towers over many other plants, standing up like a miniature palm tree, with whorl upon whorl of green foliage striped with white bands and lines. It's completely variegated from stem to leaf, and up to fifteen inches high. Put a couple of these in a spot at the edge of the border, and you are sure to be impressed. Provide fertile, evenly moist soil in full mountain sun or partial shade. Plant some specimens around the edge of a pond or even use it as a container plant. I've tried growing it for years, but while doing well in the Zone 7 winters we have for one or two years, it succumbs when we get our revolving Zone 6 winter. In the really hot southern sun, it will prefer a half-day of shade. Do not let the plant dry out. Zones 8 to 10.

Carex plantaginea, the plantain-leaved sedge or seersucker sedge, should be one of the pop-plants in the nursery trade but for some reason this species has yet to catch on. Still, every year a few more nurseries jump on board to promote this truly charming sedge that dotes on rich, moist woods. It is found in most of eastern North America ranging

Carex plantaginea

from Quebec to Saskatchewan, south to North Carolina, northern Georgia, then on to Kentucky and Minnesota. When buying this sedge, use a nursery that does not collect in the wild, as it's on the endangered species list for many states.

It's a shame that the common name for this beauty is based on the leaf's partial resemblance to that of a common lawn weed, the plantain or white-man's-foot, *Plantago major*, (the second common name referring to the Native American belief that wherever a white man walked, this non-native weed would spring forth), found in deciduous woods from Canada south to Alabama.

This plant forms evergreen clumps with broad, almost hosta-like foliage of a soft green color and pleated like seersucker cloth. The leaves are about an inch wide and can reach a two-foot length, with purple sheaths at the base, blooming in spring with purple-striped flower spikes. They make great ground covers and desirable specimen plants. Easy and dependable even in dry shade. Especially suited for lining a woodland path, for planting by water gardens or the edges of pools, and along streams in shaded locations. Zones 5 to 8.

Carex platyphylla, the silver sedge, is another native American sedge of great beauty, featuring unusually wide leaves, sometimes up to an inch,

and a lovely silvery-blue color. The species name is Greek for "having wide leaves." As a slow-spreading ground cover, with its eight- to twelve-inch height, it makes a valuable addition to mixing into a woodland garden or even growing in a container. Native to much of the eastern part of the country, like the plantain-leaved sedge, it's on the endangered list for several states.

Cultural demands are few, with well-drained soil high on the list. Once established, plants will adapt to dry conditions. Propagate by division and by seed. Zones 4 to 8.

Carex platyphylla

Carex secta is a native sedge of New Zealand where it's known as pukio. In native haunts it grows along stream banks, deep in swamps, and is fond of most damp places. This sedge sports long, graceful, very narrow, weeping, yellowish-green leaves up to six feet long, making a rather large fountain, especially attractive in a slight breeze. But according to Chiltern Seeds, the plants form large tussocks that bear three-foot flower panicles in the summer. This is followed by, and I quote from the catalog, "[in] a strange and unique manner, the matted roots and decaying leaves combine eventually to produce huge, broad, conspicuous pillars that can reach five feet in height and bodily lift the plant itself above its original home." Now that's worth waiting for, especially as this sedge grows beautifully from seed. Zones 7 to 9.

Carex siderosticha 'Island Brocade'

Carex siderosticha 'Lemon Zest'

Carex siderosticha is listed in my copy of *Flora of Japan* as a rather common sedge found growing in mountain woods from Japan to Korea, Manchuria, and on to China. But four cultivars are simply smashing additions to any garden and all are spectacular ground covers. In their leaf size, these plants resemble the plantain-leaved sedge (*Carex plantaginea*), but lack the pleated, seersucker look of those particular leaves. They are also mostly deciduous in my Asheville garden. These cultivars do best in rich, wooded, and damp soil, with partial shade. They must never be allowed to dry out.

The first cultivar is **'Banana Boat'**, a wide-leaved sedge that boasts a bold yellow-gold center strip, bounded on both sides with green. The only problem is that it's deciduous and won't come up in your garden until the soil is truly warm. The height, at best, is about nine inches. Zones 6 to 8.

The second is **'Island Brocade'**, a grand ground cover that looks more like a fledgling hosta than a sedge, with broad blades of lime green edged with golden yellow. It is exuberant in the right location but never invasive. Zones 6 to 9.

The third is **'Lemon Zest'**, brought back from Japan by that intrepid hort-traveler, Dan Hinkley, who describes it in the Heronswood Nursery catalog as "[a] superb selection of sedge proffering mounding clumps of broad lance-shaped leaves with a solid golden yellow variegation, excellent combined, in partially shaded conditions or the shaded container, with ferns, tricyrtis, Solomon's seals, etc., etc., etc."

The fourth is **'Variegata'**, a white-variegated form that Peter Gentling gave me a few years ago that has done beautifully growing in a shallow space between an ascending stone wall and a descending stone wall. There, between a small

Carex siderosticha 'Variegata'

basin full of sea oats (*Chasmanthium latifolium*) and a mass of Lenten roses (*Helleborus orientalis*), broad blades of icy white and green (with just a touch of pink at the base) sport their colors to all passers-by. Zones 5 to 9.

Carex sylvatica, the forest or sylvan sedge, with the species name from the Latin word for "forest," is a native of Eurasia where it's found growing on moist and shaded forest floors. A clumping, semi-evergreen sedge, the fourth-inch-wide, medium green leaves form dense tufts up to two feet long. In mid-spring, long, fine-textured flowers appear on wiry stems, producing long, drooping fruits on arching spikes. This sedge makes a good ground cover and is especially attractive when planted at the edge of a stream or pondside. Provide a rich, moist, fertile soil with light shade, although the leaves will take a great deal of sun if there's plenty of water. Propagate by seed or division. Zones 7 to 9.

Carex testacea, the orange New Zealand Sedge, is a perennial native of that country that grows in coastal sand dunes and the tougher parts of the interior. The plants reach a height of twelve to eighteen inches with elegant and weeping, fine olive-green leaves that turn a rich orange-brown when exposed to full sun. The flower spikes are dark brown. In most gardens plant this sedge in regular, moist to wet garden soil. In winter the orange color becomes more intense. Propagation is by seed or division. Like *Carex buchananii*, this sedge is great for containers. Zones 7 to 8.

Carex × 'The Beatles' might be a cross between C. *digitata* and C. *ornithipoda*, with the cultivar name referring to the plant's un-questionable resemblance to rock hairdos first popular in the 1960s when The Beatles ruled. Some list it as a cultivar of C. *caryophyllea*. The typical carex leaves are up to an eighth of an inch wide and usually reach a four-inch height, and resemble an overhead view of a head with plenty of hair. It's a great ground cover for rock gardens, does well in pots, and is an all-around good addition to the smaller landscape. It is sterile, so the only method of reproduction is by division. Zones 7 to 9.

Carex trifida, or the mutton-bird sedge, is one of the newer New Zealand sedges to hit the market. The species name means "three cleft," referring to marks on the seedpod. The plant makes dense, light green mounds of one-inch wide evergreen leaves, up to six feet long, that appear to be double folds with a blue-gray color on the reverse side. In midsummer, they send up nodding, cylindrical, chestnut-brown flower spikes. It's an excellent choice for a ground cover in shade and grows easily from seed. Provide sun to partial shade in moist but well-drained soil.

The *Carex* Lawn

This is not a book on lawns and lawn plants because I've never been fond of a lawn unless it surrounds a baronial castle or grand estate. My lawn, for example, has always been a mix of grasses, naturalized bulbs, and just plain weeds. That's because I rarely have the time necessary to kill the weeds and I rally against chemical lawn companies and all they represent.

But there's another kind of lawn that I first ran across in one of the stellar publications of the Brooklyn Botanic Garden. In this case it was John Greenlee writing about "Sedge Lawns for Every Landscape" in *Easy Lawns: Low Maintenance Native Grasses for Gardeners Everywhere*. So, I called John to ask a few questions. John, of course, was generous and helpful, ready to provide information on just about everything in the world of ornamental grasses, including questions referring to that marvelous new concept, the sedge lawn.

"Sedge lawns," he said, "are something new under the sun. Sedges are close botanical cousins of the grasses and to untrained eyes, look a lot like them. When properly selected and planted they really become substitutes for the traditional—and time consuming—American lawn."

"So sedges," I asked, "have many of the virtues of most native plants?"

"Right. They require little or no fertilizing, or chemicals, and many need less water for growth than many of the conventional turf grasses. And sedge lawns bring back some of the character found with the native sods that existed in this country before agriculture and unbridled development transformed the American landscape.

"Remember, most of those conventional lawn grasses came from Africa, Asia, Europe, and other parts of the world. These exotic, high-maintenance species have largely replaced our homegrown sods of native sedges and grasses. Today there's little left of those native sods and perhaps the new sedge lawn is the original sod just waiting to be discovered.

"We've selected these five sedges for their compact growth and their great green color, plus the fact that most of them are evergreen, too. Plus many will tolerate varying degrees of shade and root competition from trees. While they're best grown in their native haunts, most have shown an amazing ability to adapt to regions outside of their native range.

"And all of this promise before many new species are collected, then tested, by horticulturists and nurseries, not to mention future hybridizing and the search for new cultivars."

The five sedges that Greenlee selected as having excellent potential as substitutes for traditional lawns are Catlin sedge (*Carex texensis*), Texas Hill Country sedge (*C. perdentata*), Baltimore sedge (*C. senta*),

Pennsylvania sedge (*C. pensylvanica*), and California meadow sedge (*C. pansa*).

Carex texensis, or the Catlin sedge, is a native American ranging from Texas through Ohio, and naturalized in parts of Southern California. Greenlee bestowed the name after Southern California horticulturalist Jack Catlin, who used this plant as a companion plant for bonsai and other container plantings. Like several other types of plants, including goldenrods and oaks, these sedges easily hybridize, mingling with similar species throughout the Southwest. So it has adapted to various climates, ranging from the hot and muggy Southeast to the hot and dry Southwest. Catlin sedge forms a mat-like clump, from three to four inches high and six inches wide and needs two to three mowings a year. A dark green color in the shade, leaves turn a lighter green in full sun and need ample water to look their best. This sedge makes a fine lawn, mowed or unmowed. Plant from seed or use plugs set on six-inch centers. Zones 6 to 10.

Carex perdentata, Texas Hill Country sedge, is both drought and moisture tolerant, looking its best when watered regularly but, like most sedges, it tolerates periods of summer drought. The soft green foliage springs from roots that are almost clump forming, but slowly creep along, growing up to six inches high. A versatile plant, this sedge does equally well in sun or shade and on heavy or sandy soils. The evergreen foliage is dependably hardy to Zone 6 (and possibly lower). In spring or fall, plant from plugs on six- or twelve-inch centers.

Carex pensylvanica, the yellow sedge, is a well-known carex found in many places around the country. As Greenlee notes, here is a sedge that, using hybridization, should hold much

134

promise for the natural lawn of the future. As we write, many nurseries and horticulturists are evaluating clones and cultivars from shore to shore. Typically yellow sedge grows on sandy soil in dappled shade or as a constituent of low prairies, so plants can tolerate less than ideal conditions in the garden. Noninvasive, its creeping roots form dense mats of medium green, fine-textured foliage growing about six to eight inches high when not mowed. If mowed, cut two or three times a year at a cutting height of three to four inches. In spring or fall, plant plugs on six- or twelve-inch centers.

Carex pansa [*Carex arenicola*], the California meadow sedge, is proclaimed by Greenlee as one of the finest native sedges for natural lawns. Largely untested in the East, plants have proven durable in Texas and Colorado, their slowly creeping, dark green foliage maintaining a four- to six-inch height without mowing. Mowing two or three times a year keeps the foliage low, tight, and like a traditional lawn. This meadow sedge will tolerate various soil conditions and temperatures, ranging from sandy, exposed seacoasts to heavy clays and hot, inland valleys. It's also fairly tolerant of foot traffic. Doing well in either full sun or partial shade, it will thin out in deep shade. Plant plugs six to twelve inches on center.

Carex senta, the Baltimore sedge, is described by Greenlee as a more refined version of the Catlin sedge. They are identical except for the shorter flower spikes on *C. senta*. The Baltimore sedge makes a neater and more lawn-like appearance when left unmowed. Originally discovered by Briar Hoffman, this plant was found growing in a church lawn in Towson, Maryland. It's one of the best-growing sedges for a lawn in deep shade. Treat this sedge like *C. texensis*.

Greenlee explains, "Because, the seeds of many sedges are short-lived and have low germination rates, these lawns are usually started by using plugs. And," he added with fervor, "the most important step in establishing a new sedge lawn is to start with weed-free soil. So, if you are converting an old lawn from grasses to sedges, you must be absolutely sure that the old lawn is either dead or completely removed."

That is accomplished by one or a combination of the following methods: repeat tilling, sod-cutting, smothering, or, if all else fails, an herbicide. If you choose tilling you must plow up the soil two or three times, with each use of the tiller about a week apart.

Sod-cutters are an esoteric piece of power equipment that I first saw on the British garden show, *Ground Force*. This machine will strip off the top layer of grass and roots found in an established lawn, leaving in its wake a nearly weed-free area. Finally (because there are no truly safe herbicides to remove an area such as a lawn), you can smother a lawn (and the accompanying weeds), by laying sheets of black plastic, or old sheets of cardboard (like refrigerators are packed in), leaving the cover on the lawn for an entire season.

Once a *Carex*, Now a Loner

Cymophyllus fraseri, or Fraser's sedge, named for John Fraser (1750–1811), the famous Scottish botanist, once belonged to the Carex Clan but moved to its own genus because of botanical differences. It's native to the southern Appalachian Mountains and is also known as the lily-leaf sedge. The genus refers to the Greek *cyma* or "wave" and *phyllon*, or "leaf," from the minutely undulate margins.

Here's a perennial sedge with beautiful strap-like basal leaves and plants that grow larger in circumference with age. They bloom in very early spring with white spikes of flowers on stalks up to two feet high. In John Cram's next-door garden a mature clump of this plant has been blooming in late March for decades, surrounded by emerging whippoorwill flowers (*Trillium cuneatum*) and burgeoning ferns. As the trilliums fade, Fraser's sedge then demands your complete attention.

A bit fussy about location, Fraser's sedge deserves all the help you can provide, beginning with a soil rich in humus and with adequate moisture. It does not grow in water, but the roots will reach for it, so a great place for this sedge is along the low banks of a stream or beside a pond. My long-time garden friend Bebe Miles suggests that if it doesn't rain or the surrounding terrain is not damp enough, be prepared to water this plant to guarantee survival. Zones 7 and 8.

Cymophyllus fraseri

The *Cyperus* Clan

The genus name *Cyperus* is from the Greek *cypeiros*, the ancient name for these plants. About 600 species, mostly perennials, are native to both the tropic and temperate zones and rarely found where weather is truly cold. The leaves are narrow and grass-like, the culms simple or compound and usually known as trigonous, or three-sided, like the sedges. Flowers are bisexual, with linear spikelets appearing in branched umbels of panicles, followed by a three-angled fruit or a compressed nut. In general, propagation is by division or by seed.

The species mentioned here are all marvelous additions to the water garden and bring a touch of the exotic to backyard gardening. Most are used for their decorative assets and while they can be planted directly at a pond margin, are at their best when grown in pots placed in the water, using a mix of garden loam, sharp sand, and some additional peat moss. Note: You can prevent muddying the water with displaced potting soil by covering the top of the planted pots with a layer of gravel or pea gravel, then gently lowering the pots into the water garden.

Cyperus albostriatus, the dwarf umbrella palm or umbrella sedge, originally came from Africa and the West Indies and has become a favorite aquatic herb used as a houseplant—or planted in water gardens or, in Zone 10, outdoors. This is an attractive plant that has been in cultivation for well over 200 years, and, thanks to the spikelets that cluster on top of the leaves, this *Cyperus* looks as tropical as it is. Height is up to three feet. This plant is semi-aquatic, preferring damp soil or even complete submergence. When growing in pots, remember to keep the potting mix moist but never let the plants sit in standing water. Regardless of its tropical appearance, this is a plant that likes its heat tempered with shade; full sun can scorch the leaves. Zones 9 and 10.

Cyperus albostriatus **'Nanus'** is the dwarf form of this umbrella plant, usually growing no taller than sixteen inches.

Cyperus albostriatus **'Variegatus'** is a brilliantly variegated cultivar with leaves longitudinally striped with colors of light cream or pale yellow.

Cyperus alternifolius, the umbrella palm, Nile-grass, or umbrella plant, is a native of Africa and the West Indies. The species name refers to

Cyperus albostriatus

the overlapping whorl of v-shaped leaves at the top of the slender culms. The culms grow up to a height of three feet and form clumps up to five feet across. The leaf-like bracts at the top of the stem whorl around like the ribs on an umbrella—and it's a showstopper plant when the leaves are themselves topped with flat clusters of greenish flowers that turn brown with age. Like *C. albostriatus*, these plants can be sunburned, so a half-day of shade is recommended, but they will take heat with ease as long as the roots have water. Propagate by division or seed. Zones 9 and 10.

Cyperus alternifolius **'Variegatus'** has culms streaked with white and bracts that range from having longitudinal striping to being entirely white.

Cyperus esculentus, commonly known as chufa or nut grass, is included in this list because when the proper conditions exist, it often crops up as a weed. Unfortunately, this is one of those few occasions when a plant is called a weed even though it has paid its dues to humanity many times over. The species name means "edible" and edible they are, as the tubers are eaten boiled or raw, cooked or candied, roasted or blanched, and added to many foods, especially soups. In spite of these virtues, this native of both North America and Eurasia is often included in the list of America's Five Worst Weeds.

Chufa has for centuries been used as an edible tuber, with popular names such as edible galingale, earth-almond, coco sedge, and rush-nut. The "nuts" are reputed to taste similar to almonds and can be eaten raw or cooked with recipes abounding. It's a perennial with slender rhizomes that end in nearly round tubers. Like all sedges, the stem is triangular in cross section. Height is about three feet. The foliage is a pleasant mid-green, topped with very ornamental flower heads consisting of numerous flat spikelets, usually straw colored or yellowish brown. The plants do well in pots, too.

In spite of its being attractive, most homeowners object to this plant for its invasive tendencies and would like it removed from the backyard. The best way is to pull up the plants by hand as soon as the leaves are seen, checking back every few weeks to see that you've gotten it all. For removal of large areas of chufa, check with your local Extension service, because the chemicals needed are usually not within the purview of the average homeowner.

Cyperus giganteus 'Mexico' is probably a cultivar of the species, a native of Mexico and similar to the species C. *papyrus* in most aspects, differing only in minor floral characteristics. I saw the plant in the indoor water garden at Brookside Gardens, located just a few miles from Washington, D.C., in Wheaton, Maryland, and was quite impressed by its beauty and the fullness of the flowering branches. Zone 9.

Cyperus haspan [Cyperus isocladus], or dwarf papyrus, is an elegant member of the umbrella plants, its attractiveness due mostly to the clustered spikelets that resemble small shooting stars. The culms reach a height of two to three feet. It's a native of wetlands in the southern United States and Central America. Best as a houseplant, it can be set outdoors only in the warmest parts of the country. Usually it tops twenty inches. If grown outside, plants do well in shallow water, or, when grown in pots, by keeping the pot base in a saucer of water. Provide full sun to light shade. Amazingly, the plants propagate when the culms bend and the flower heads touch water. Zones 8 to 10.

Cyperus haspan

Cyperus papyrus, or Egyptian papyrus, also called the Egyptian paper plant, is the famous species of ancient renown used in the manufacture of paper from about 2750 B.C. until the invention of the wood pulp process. Note that the species name is a variant on the word "paper." If the local stationery shop is out of something to write on, the process of making paper from papyrus involves taking thin, wet strips of the pith from flowering stems, laying them so the edges slightly overlap, then crossing them with additional strips, and finally drying the sheets under weights. Papyrus is also used to thatch roofs and, in a warmer climate than our mountain hideouts, lasts a long time before breaking down. Sailors of the Mediterranean Sea in the old days made rafts by tying the stems together in bundles. And if there's

Cyperus papyrus

the rhizomes are always under water. Temperatures should be kept above 60° F, but I've grown this plant in a cool greenhouse where water temperatures were usually around 50° F, though I doubt if the plant was very happy. Start plants in clay pots and use a soil mix of one-third each of potting soil, composted manure, and sand. And remember, this plant wants full sun. It can survive a mild winter (Zone 7) if under a few feet of water, but in colder areas bring plants into a warmer place for the winter.

Bringing them in for the winter isn't as hard to do as it sounds, if you grow the plant in one pot then set it in another. Any reasonably warm spot will do as long as the temperature stays above freezing.

little else to do around the house, you can use the stems and leaves to distill alcohol. Not only that, but this papyrus is the same plant that surrounded the baby Moses when he was discovered by Pharaoh's daughter. In your backyard it will probably reach a height of about twelve feet, but gets up to fifteen feet when back home on the Nile.

Plants were first brought to England in 1803. So it hasn't been used in garden pools for very long, at least when you consider its long history. The basal leaves of this plant have been reduced to small brown sheaths on the triangular stems— remember, hollow stems are usually grass, solid stems are rushes, and triangular stems are the sedges. What look like leaves are really bracts that cluster at the top of the stem and surround spikes that end in scale-like flowers.

You can grow papyrus in an indoor or outdoor pool, or even in a pot set in a larger container, so

Baumea rubiginosa var. *variegata*

Other Members of the Family
Baumea rubiginosa* var. *variegata is an Australian native rush that has rounded, flat, green leaves with yellow and darker green variegations along the edges. The generic name probably comes from an Australian botanist named Baum, and the species name means "rusty red." The leathery leaves emerge from a slit in the previous leaf, beginning as cylindrical, but ending up flat—a teardrop shape in cross-section. They grow from one to two feet tall and are evergreen. Grow these plants in water at a depth of one to six inches, in sun or partial shade. Divide the clumps in spring. Zones 7 to 11.

Dichromena latifolia

Dichromena latifolia [*Rhynchospora latifolia*], or white star grass, is an American relative of what is basically a tropical branch of the sedge family. It is found from southeast Virginia to Florida, west to Texas, and in the West Indies and Mexico. It dotes on broad, damp savannahs and marshes, where it forms sizeable clumps of foliage. A new planting can make a three-foot clump in three years and will produce fifteen-inch stalks topped with spectacular white bracts (in reality modified leaves) that surround tiny flowers. It will survive in dry places but excels when boggy conditions prevail. I solved the problem by planting mine over a plastic dishpan. The genus is from the Greek *dis*, or "double," and *chroma*, or "color," referring to the bicolored bracts; *latifolia* means "broad leaves." Zones 7 to 10.

The Spike Rushes
Eleocharis, or the spike rush, is a cosmopolitan genus of some 200 species, many of which grow in marshes or shallow bodies of water. The generic name is from the Greek, *elos*, or "marsh," and *charis*, or "grace," as these plants do bring great beauty to wetlands. Botany books describe these plants as being quite variable both in height and the thickness of the culms, not to mention the size of the spikelets, all usually attributed to available water supply. Leaves have been reduced to bladeless sheathes surrounding the lower part of the culms. That said, many of the species are very attractive, living up to their generic name.

The nurseries that stock this plant are few and far between but, like the field rush, it's often found near bodies of water. If you have permission, take a few and be surprised at how they can dress up a water garden.

Eleocharis acicularis, the needle spike rush, is a ubiquitous plant found just about everywhere in North America, apparently drawing the line just north of Central Florida. It grows at the edges of ponds, lakes, and slow-moving shallow streams, even in wet meadows, differing from the rest of the spike rushes in its small size.

The solid, not hollow, leaves are very thin and cylindrical, arising from runners. Little bunches surface about every inch and when grown in a small container, become as thick as a shaggy green carpet. Flowers are tiny and followed by little sharply pointed spikelets, each about a millimeter long.

I have a glazed green pottery container measuring six inches square housing a cluster of plants, which closely resemble poorly cut green hair. The pot is always kept in a saucer of water. This extremely cute plant always elicits comments from visitors. Zones 3 to 9.

Eleocharis parvula, the spike rush, or, as it's often called, hair grass, is a wide-ranging plant growing in saline soil along the coast from Newfoundland to Florida and Texas, then traveling inland to New York, Michigan, and Missouri; it's also found in South America, Cuba, Africa, and Europe.

These grass-like perennials are easily recognized by the brownish flowering spikes at the tops of the smooth, round stems. They are also important plants for wildlife as they provide habitat for waterfowl and small mammals. Propagate by seed and by division.

Eleocharis acicularis

Eleocharis parvula

141

The Bulrushes

Scirpus is the old Latin name used by Pliny to designate a bulrush, although the bulrush is really a sedge. *Scirpus* is a genus of about 200 species of annual or perennial herbs that typically grow in or near shallow water. The culms are usually erect and sheathed at the base, while the leaves are very small blades or reduced to those aforementioned sheaths at the base of the culm.

Scirpus cernuus, the miniature bulrush or fiber optic grass, is a sedge that has enjoyed great success, not only in the garden but as a houseplant, too. Other common names include electric grass and the fountain bulrush. Older books call it *Eleocharis cernuus* or *Isolepis gracilis* (*Isolepis* means "having equal scales" and refers to the primitive leaves), but no matter the scientific name, this plant looks for all the world like a novelty item that might be advertised in the *National Enquirer*. The specific scientific name of *cernuus* means "slightly drooping," and that the stems do. Originally from the East Indies, it's naturalized in southern Europe, and this graceful tufted plant, growing to a height of eight to twelve inches, has found a home on European windowsills for decades. Unlike many houseplants, this one can exist without sun or very bright light and manages to survive in a north window. Numerous round, threadlike, glossy, fresh green stems become pendant as they mature, and are then graced with little white flower heads.

Usually called an annual, it's a perennial that does not like a chill. When temperatures fall below 55° F for any length of time, let the plant rest, watering only enough to keep the soil from completely drying out. With age, the plants become tussocks, with the new leaves

Scirpus cernuus

arising from the dead foliage. In addition to growing in a pot, this plant is great at the water's edge or in a shallow pond, especially where the leaves can weep over the edges of some attractive rocks. Remember to provide some shade where the sun is really hot. After a year, you can give the plants a haircut, shearing about two inches above the crown. Propagation is by division or by seed. Zones 9 and 10.

Scirpus cyperinus, or wool-grass, is a favorite plant of mine because it grew in the marshes at the end of our lake when we lived in the Catskill Mountains. The culms are bright green, usually between four and six feet tall, and support a terminal inflorescence consisting of spikelets that are eventually covered with wooly threads (they are excellent in dried flower arrangements). While not sleek

142

Scirpus cyperinus

spikes for food and the stems for baskets and rugs. These plants are also valuable for wildlife as nesting locations and today they are used for stabilizing banks from erosion and to treat contaminated water. Propagation is by division or by seeds. Provide full sun. Zones 5 to 10.

***Scirpus tabernaemontani* 'Zebrinus'**, the striped bulrush or porcupine plant, has culms striped with light yellow bands on three to five foot stems. They want partial sun and plenty of water. These plants can also be grown indoors if there is plenty of light. Any culms that revert to pure green should be removed. Zones 5 to 9.

enough for the formal water or bog garden, they are perfect for naturalizing in the wild garden. Zones 5 to 9.

***Scirpus tabernaemontani*,** the soft-stem bulrush, is a tall perennial plant, sometimes reaching a height of nine feet, consisting of round, almost spongy culms that come to a point. Several to many flowers appear in spikelets that emerge from the culms. Plants grow in shallow water at the margins of streams, lakes, and ponds and spread by seed or by creeping rhizomes.

The specific name is from *tabernae*, a Latin word for "a temporary shelter" and *montani* for "mountains," and refers to Native Americans using the woven stems to make lean-tos, in addition to using the roots, pollen, and flower

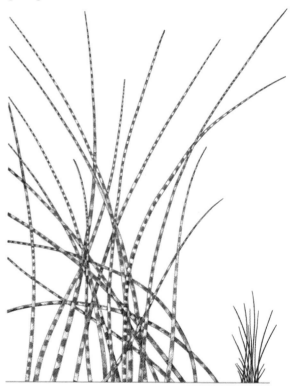

Scirpus tabernaemontani 'Zebrinus'

Cotton Grass

About twenty species of cotton grass are native to the Northern Hemisphere. Most are not worthy of garden attention but three species definitely are. The scientific name *Eriophorum* is derived from the Greek, *erion*, for "wool" or "cotton" and *phoros*, meaning "bearing," all referring to the cottony spikelets.

I hesitate to mention *Eriophorum callitrix*, or hare's-tail grass, and *E. polystachion*, cotton grass or cotton rush, because neither of these plants is happy in the heat of a Southeast summer. They are plants of fresh meadows, swamps, marshes, and bogs, and native to Asia. They are grown for their white feathery seedheads, with long bristles that, with a bit of imagination, could be the tail of a hare. They do well at the water's edge and, unlike other types of cotton grass, are not very invasive.

Eriophorum virginicum, or tawny cotton grass, is happier in warmer climes. This is an upright and spreading perennial with a strong root system and bearing neat tufts of cotton-like bristles at the stem tips. The flowers actually resemble cotton balls, looking as though they were recently pulled from a bottle of vitamins, tawny white and changing to a coppery color at the base. The leaves are narrow and flat, with the plant height up to four, sometimes five, feet tall. The stems, like those of other sedges, are triangular in cross-section. Plants are at home in peaty soils and poorly drained areas, and are often found in cranberry bogs. Zones 6 to the colder parts of Zone 9.

The Rushes

Rushes belong to a very small family of plants, the Juncaceae, consisting of some eight or nine genera of sedge-like plants of wide distribution. *Juncos* is the ancient Latin name for these plants and was derived from *jungere*, "to join," referring to the use of the stems to tie or band other articles together.

Most of the rushes come from cold and barren lands and differ from the sedges in having six petals in a flower rather than none. But like the sedges, their main value to nature is in binding the soil.

In spite of their lowly place in the plant world, they have a few notable uses for mankind, including one that lasted throughout most of English history. Before the general use of carpets, rushes were gathered, mixed with herbs and flowers, then strewn upon the floors of castle and cottage alike, to brighten things up and to keep litter from grinding into dirt floors.

The country folk had the local wetlands and swamps as a source of these plants, but the cities,

Juncus effusus and *Juncus effusus* 'Spiralis'

144

like London during Elizabethan days, were forced to import rushes. By the time carting charges were paid, these trifles for the floors of the well-off city dweller could be very expensive. One of the charges of extravagance leveled against Cardinal Wolsey was "he caused his floors to be strewn with rushes too frequently." Because table manners in those days were not of the best, and animals were often fed at the table, not to mention the presence of the master's dogs sleeping at his feet, the floor rushes quickly became unwholesome, and the cardinal can hardly be faulted for changing them whenever he could.

Later, large rush-carts were constructed of rushes staked onto wagons, with a hole at the top for a young man to sit beneath and thrust a living tree through the opening. The wagons were often covered with white cloths and decorated with borrowed treasures such as silver tankards and cream jugs, then adorned with brightly colored ribbons. These carts were preceded by young men and women, their bodies covered with streaming ribbons, dancing the Morris Dance, in celebration of the "Gathering of the Rushes." (The Morris Dance was a Spanish import and originally called the Moor Dance.)

The celebration was not scheduled for spring, but in August when the rushes were being gathered for the coming winter, to be used by local churches alongside drafty doors as a protection against the cold.

The rush-cart persisted well into the nineteenth century, especially in rural villages, but has now left the scene like so many pleasant memories of the past.

Juncus effusus, the common rush, soft rush, or Japanese-mat, is a ubiquitous plant of wet and swampy conditions across much of the world. It also does quite well in overgrown pastures and forgotten fields where the soil is dry and poor.

Juncus effusus 'Spiralis'

The rootstock is of the creeping variety, and the rounded stems are a pale green, very pliant, and end in a point. There are no leaves except for a few brown wrappings at the base of the plant. Leaves can grow up to five feet tall but usually are around three feet high. The flowers occur halfway up the stems, forming side-panicles of greenish-brown spikelets. When plants are used in groups within a naturalized area, the dense clumps are most attractive and persist throughout the winter. Many of the stems turn a bright rust-red in the fall. Note: If you peel the green outer layer of the stem, just like pulling a zipper, you'll find a center core of white pith. Years ago, this was dried, then tied with others, soaked in kitchen grease, and lighted for rush candles. The pith was also used for candlewicks.

Rushes do well in pots but must be in water up to the level of the top dressing of dirt. And the water should be changed every few weeks to prevent the soil from becoming sour.

Common rushes are quite beautiful in the water garden, planted along the edges of streams and ponds. They do very well in full sun or light shade, their roots in water. Remember, the variegated types need some shade to prevent burning. Propagation is by division or by seed. Zones 5 to 8.

Juncus effusus 'Aureus Striatus' has its stems banded with yellow-green, the stems reaching a height of three feet.

Juncus effusus 'Blonde Ambition', known as the golden corkscrew rush, was a 2002 plant introduction from Bill and Dianna Janssen of Collector's Nursery in Battleground, Washington, as reported by Tony Avent of Plant Delights Nursery. These curlicues are about eight inches tall and eighteen inches wide, making a mound of corkscrew straws in tones of golden yellow and green—from a distance one might say chartreuse. Conditions require partial shade and a slightly moist soil, and it seems to be hardy from Zones 4 to 9.

Juncus effusus 'Carman's Japanese' is a very ornamental species of rush from a selection made by Ed Carman of Los Gatos, California. This particular cultivar is known for the showy, tawny-colored flower clusters that form at the tips of the cylindrical leaves, usually so heavy that the leaves bend to the ground in a most beautiful manner. Zones 7 to 9.

Juncus effusus var. pacificus 'Quartz Creek' is a selection made in Quartz Creek, Oregon, by the Native Sons Nursery of California. The lime-green color is very bright, especially since the eighteen-inch leaves spring forth from dark chocolate-colored basal sheaths. These plants are great in water gardens or, as I have them, in a beautiful pot. Although they are slow spreaders, they eventually can form dense colonies, as long as they have water and full sun or partial shade. Zones 6 to 9.

Juncus effusus var. pacificus 'Quartz Creek'

Juncus effusus 'Spiralis', the spiral rush, grows up to eighteen inches or more in height, but usually the twisted stems fall back to the ground in a tangled mass. It's especially effective in a pot raised above the ground so the corkscrew stems can tumble down the sides. When happy, a plant can eventually grow to a two-foot diameter. If this plant is set in the middle of other plants, it looks like a convention of worms taking a well-deserved nap after overlong discussions.

Juncus effusus 'Vittatus' has stems narrowly striped with pure white and green. It, too, reaches a height of three feet.

Juncus effusus **'Zebrinus'** usually stops growing at thirty inches, with stems broadly striped a greenish white.

Juncus inflexus **'Afro'**, or the Blue Medusa rush, is an intricate gem great for growing by pondside or in any moist area. Crowds of tightly spiraled, glossy blue-gray stems are thrown up from the central base, appearing like out-of-control corkscrews, and frequently dusted in a bloom so they resemble bronze firecrackers. Plants are similar to *Juncus effusus* 'Spiralis' except for the blue-gray foliage, also growing to a one- to two-foot height. Here's an excellent accent plant for around the edge of a pond. This rush is evergreen in milder climates. For best results, provide a

Juncus patens 'Carman's Gray'

moist, well-drained soil in full sun or partial shade. Plants can also do well in up to three inches of water or in boggy soil. This is the best corkscrew rush for hot climates. Zones 5 to 10.

Juncus patens **'Carman's Gray'**, or the California gray rush, is another selection of a native rush made by Ed Carman of Los Gatos. The plants grow about two feet high, with a stiff, vertical habit and typical small bunches of flowers appearing at the tips of the cylindrical leaves. It's reported to be more heat tolerant than the other rushes, doing well throughout California.

Juncus patens **'Elk Blue'**, a striking rush with exceptional evergreen blue foliage, is a strong grower. The flowers that appear on the stem tops

Juncus inflexus 'Afro'

are the color of rich, dark chocolate and a lovely sight when contrasting with the blue. They begin to appear in midsummer and last through to fall. Use this rush along the edge of a pond or stream, or in a special pot on your deck or patio. The best color is achieved in the sun, using average to wet soil. Height is about two feet.

The Woodrushes

Woodrushes comprise about eighty species of perennial herbs belonging to the genus *Luzula*, which is from the Latin for "glow-worm." The name refers to the shining drops of dew clinging to the silvery hairs that adorn many a woodrush leaf. They are native to the cold and temperate regions of the world, especially Eurasia.

For all their lack of garden fame, woodrushes are marvelous plants of great beauty, perfect as ground covers; the leaves edged with those silvery hairs are truly beautiful.

Luzula nivea

Luzula nivea, the showy woodrush, originally came from the mountains of central Europe. It's a delightful, tufted grass that grows high up in the Alps, and in summer bears clusters of white, spiky, fluffy flowers in loose, arching panicles. Using stoloniferous roots, this slowly spreading evergreen

perennial forms loose clumps of flat, green leaves three-fourths of an inch wide with finely haired margins, from twelve to sixteen inches high. The flowers are on two-foot stems and will eventually turn brown and persist. A shaded location and a moist soil are necessary for best growth. That tolerance for moist soils makes the showy woodrush useful near ponds or other water features, and it's perfect for boggy areas. Propagation is by division or by seed. Zones 6 to 9.

Luzula nivea 'Marginata' is a beautiful cultivar with the leaf edges lightly banded with white.

Luzula nivea 'Ruby Stiletto'

Luzula nivea 'Ruby Stiletto' makes an attractive mound of ruby-tinted foliage in late winter and early spring.

Luzula pilosa, the hairy woodrush, is, as its common name suggests, a perennial herb with dark green leaves edged with silver hairs. In our garden it's a wildflower, seeding about with fruits from dark chestnut brown flowers that bloom from April to June. These plants look their best when massed as woodland ground covers, delighting in a wooded and shaded location. Propagate by division or by seed. Zones 5 to 8.

Luzula pilosa

Luzula sylvatica, the greater woodrush, grows about a foot high but in flower extends up to two feet. It's a low-growing evergreen ground cover that spreads by runners. The leaves are dark green, about a half inch wide, and a foot long. Plants prefer partial to full shade, blooming in the spring with chestnut brown spike-like flowers that may be cut away after blooming or left for their winter interest. Provide partial to full shade. Propagation is by division or by seed.

***Luzula sylvatica* 'Aurea'** has chartreuse leaves and is not very cold tolerant. Small, chestnut-brown flowers bloom from mid-spring to early summer. Use as a ground cover in a mixed border or in a woodland garden. Grow in poor to moderately fertile, moist, well-drained soil in partial or deep shade. I have one of these plants set beneath the shade of a dwarf redwood (*Sequoia sempervirens* 'Adpressa') where it shines in the late afternoon twilight like a many-flamed golden candle.

***Luzula sylvatica* 'Variegata'** has one-foot leaves with a thin, creamy-white edge and

open sprays of golden-yellow flowers on eighteen-inch stems.

The Horsetails

The horsetails, members of the genus *Equisetum*, are the direct descendents of plants that grew on earth millions of years ago during the Carboniferous Period of geologic time. The vast American coalfields were formed as mounds of this and other vegetation sank ever deeper into the mire and through chemical action eventually became great veins of coal. At that time in earth's history, dragonflies sported fourteen-inch wingspans and flitted about misty swamps, alighting on ferns with fronds that rose thirty feet into a sky filled with scuttling clouds and smoke from a legion of volcanoes.

Today horsetails have diminished in size, the largest rarely topping six feet and the smallest

Horsetails with coleus.

measured in inches. The scientific name is from the Latin, *equus*, "horse," and *seta*, "bristle," referring to the plant's resemblance to a horse's tail, especially since many of the species produce stems covered with whorled branchlets. Horsetails grow along streams, lakes, and ditches.

Evergreen shoots grow from a perennial rhizome and have such high silica content that in pioneer days they were used to clean and polish pots and pans. Railroad cooks would use a bunch of stems to clean up the breakfast frying pan, then toss them out the window, hence these plants are found growing along gravel railroad beds throughout the country.

The cone-like caps that top the ringed stems produce spores, not seeds, and follow a complicated reproductive cycle like the ferns. Spores produce small, green, lobed prothalli that manufacture both male and female cells, which eventually meet to create a new plant. The tiny pennants that circle the rings, which in turn section off the stems, are primitive, scale-like leaves, so the major part of photosynthesis occurs in the stem. Individual stem sections can be pulled apart and sometimes can be put back together again.

Equisetum hyemale

Equisetum hyemale does quite well in a pot where it can spend the summer in the pool or at the water's edge. If planted directly in the garden,

they spread with amazing energy, each piece of a plant's rhizome capable of creating a new plant. When bounded by an impenetrable barrier, these plants make a fascinating ground cover unlike any other plant on the market. At a gigantic supermarket called Jungle Jim's, in Hamilton, Ohio, on the divided road leading to the parking lot the landscape architects used common horsetail as a ground cover to fill the three-foot wide, curbed median between the pavements.

The species name of *hyemale* means "like winter," pointing out the absence of leaves on the stems. Height is about two feet but can range up to five feet. Provide wet and fertile soil in full sun. Propagate by division most any time of the year. Zones 5 to 10.

Equisetum hyemale 'Robustum' is an American cultivar, often growing to a height of seven feet. When members of the local Ikebana Society visit our garden, everybody wants a sample of this giant.

Equisetum hyemale 'Robustum' with hardy begonias (*Begonia grandis*).

150

Equisetum scirpoides is the dwarf scouring rush, with threadlike stems about three inches high. It makes a great ground cover and does well in pots. Like other members of this clan, it's also invasive. Zones 5 to 10.

Equisetum scirpoides var. contorta, bears contorted stems that look like a green bunch of steel wool. It's great when growing in an attractive pot and does well between the cracks of a stone-paved walkway. It also makes a great cover for a dish garden or bonsai.

Equisetum variegatum has dark green stems with a pronounced black band on the leaves above each stem section. It grows about six inches high.

Chondropetalum tectorum

Restios at the Bottom of the World

Ever hear of a *fynbo*? If you do a Web search, you're likely to come up with a Finnish cheese. But if you persevere, you'll get an entry that refers to a fynbo as the characteristic vegetation of the southernmost end of Africa, specifically the Western Cape of South Africa. The name comes from the Old Dutch, *fijn bosch* (or in present day Dutch, *fijn bos*) meaning "a fine forest." This habitat area covers about 35,000 square miles, being slightly larger than Scotland.

Fynbo vegetation is characterized by evergreen shrubs that are usually tough and prickly (being armed with small, tough leaves) or woody plants that bear flat leathery leaves. There are few trees but a fantastic collection of magnificent flowers and bulbs, including various lilies and succulents. Summers are hot and dry with little rain, while winters have plenty of rain with frost appearing only on the mountaintops. In other words, it's a Mediterranean climate.

The vegetation includes proteas (those glorious flowers so often found in very expensive floral arrangements), heaths (*Erica* spp.), and reeds. It's the reeds in which we're interested. These plants belong to the family Restionaceae, the common name being Cape reeds or restios, with *restio* referring to the Latin *restis* meaning "cord" or "rope."

In the Great Plains of America we have the grasses, but in the fynbos, there are the reeds. They've adapted to the rains of winter and the heat of summer. Unlike the grasses, the leaves of reeds are small, dry, and brown, with the solid stems green, having taken over food manufacturing (photosynthesis). The restios look a great deal like the horsetails. Plants are dioecious, with male and female flowers on separate plants, the male plants bearing cones with pollen and female plants bearing cones with feathery stigmas to receive the pollen. Like the grasses, most of the restios are wind-pollinated and the seeds are often collected and distributed by ants. Finally, in South African nature, the restios often occur in damp and poorly drained areas, preferring a heavy, acidic soil.

Restios make good container plants.

The first restio I ever encountered was at Longwood Gardens in Kennett Square, Pennsylvania. There, in a large pot near the end of a long greenhouse, stood an amazing plant with six-foot reed-like stems that looked as though they were adorned with green fringe. I was, of course, hooked!

The following plants are members of that family. It should also be noted that the culture of restios in America is something new. Word has it that these plants are hardier than generally believed, but they cannot overwinter in cold, wet soil and certainly are not for the colder part of Zone 8 and lower zones.

Calopsis paniculata is a tall, reed-like member of the restio family, with stems often reaching a ten-foot height with an eight- to ten-foot spread. When in bloom each stem is topped with hundreds of light brown spikelets, and packs double the horticultural punch. The scientific name means "beautiful panicles" and refers to the

flower clusters. The stems and small leaves are a bright green and resemble bamboo when first emerging from the soil. These plants make great water features as they like plenty of moisture at the roots, but the soil must be well drained, especially during the winter months. The stems are used to make brooms and this is one of the most popular members of the group for thatching roofs. Zones 8 to 10.

Chondropetalum tectorum, the New Zealand sedge, begins life on the small side, but with age develops into a large specimen plant. The generic name is from the Greek *chondros*, meaning "cartilage" or "hard and tough," while *petalum* means "petal." The specific name is from the Latin *tectorum*, meaning "roofing," as this plant has a long history as a thatching material.

This practical, strange and beautiful, long-lived plant has wiry, green stems bearing small greenish flowers and closely resembles our own spike rushes (see earlier entry). Plants make wonderful container subjects and are great for low maintenance gardens.

Chondropetalum tectorum

In Africa, these plants grow naturally in marshes and seeps, built on layers of sand. Once settled in on their own turf, they can easily reach a five-foot height with up to an eight-foot spread. Again in Southern Africa, there are different cultivars of this plant, ranging in height from a few feet to eight feet high. The problem with the plant's ultimate height is its inability to withstand pruning: When stems are cut over a few years, they die.

Maintenance is simple because the only job is removing dead and decaying culms. They need full sun, a well-drained soil, and plenty of open air. Once established, they can stand long periods without water. Zones 8 to 10.

Elegia capensis, or the broom reed, is like a horsetail plant that's gone to charm school and is ready for the big time. The bamboo-like

Elegia capensis

stems are adorned (some might say festooned) with threadlike filaments of bright green and when set in motion by the wind, look like a display of dancing lights. The scientific name means "elegant plant of the Cape." Spring brings forth golden brown terminal flowers followed by dark brown seedheads. Provide full sun in moisture-rich soil. Cut back the clumps to rejuvenate them. Zones 8 to 10.

Restio tetraphyllus

Restio tetraphyllus, or the plume rush, is an Australian member (really Tasmanian) of the clan and produces dense clumps of three-foot bamboo-like stems, with each node wrapped by a light brown sheath and thin bright-green threadlike foliage beginning halfway up the stem. It appreciates acid soil and is best grown in a tub. The species name means "four-leaved." Provide a good, moist soil but like clematis, the root run is best kept cool. Zone 8 to 9.

Rhodocoma gigantea is a tall plant reaching a twelve-foot height under good growing conditions in its African home, but usually reaching about nine feet in a good American year. In the fall of the year, arching plumes of feathery bright green foliage are followed by chestnut-brown seedheads. Once again, this is a great container plant. Zones 8 to 9.

Thamnochortus insignis

Thamnochortus cinereus is a small restio from the mountains of South Africa, with plants growing three feet high. The gray-green foliage makes a stunning statement but when topped by golden-brown flowers in summer, it becomes a great specimen plant. English gardeners report that when cut down by a chilled winter, this plant, like many of its kind, will grow back in the spring, as long as the freeze hasn't affected the roots. Zones 8 and 9.

Thamnochortus insignis is unbranched and has small chocolate-brown flowers at the stem tips.

Rhodocoma gigantea

A FEW FAVORITE BAMBOOS

For me, bamboos conjure up visions of steamy jungles with orange orangutans crawling beneath masses of dark green leaves, or Chinese robber barons at war with Malayan rubber pirates, or Bette Davis in a prime role as the femme fatale in a movie such as *The Letter*.

But in today's international world of horticulture, bamboos have now achieved a prominent place as desirable landscape plants and for growing, quite handily, in containers.

For many years bamboos were listed as giant grasses. While there are similarities (both grasses and bamboos belong to the family Graminae), bamboos are usually very large, long-lived, woody, evergreen grasses with stout stems (really culms) and well-developed (and often far-ranging) root systems. Many bamboos are also monocarpic: They live only a short time after flowering, and often all clones of a particular species will flower at the same time regardless of where they are in the world.

Most bamboos are very fast spreaders, and even in colder climates some species have been known to grow more than ten feet horizontally in one month. The secret is in the food reserves contained in the roots

Pleioblastus pygmaeus

and stems. That's why they are such popular foods in the Orient.

There are two types of bamboos: the runners and the clumpers. Runners spread by sending out rhizomes at a depth of about a foot, and when hitting a barrier they can easily change direction. In one year runners can spread quite far, with their progress measured in yards. In essence, clumpers grow in upon themselves, creating a root clump that is not invasive. They do enlarge their circle of growth, but it's measured in inches. Runners make great ground covers and clumpers are especially beautiful when grown as specimens or in hedges.

And almost any bamboo can be grown in a container, even the running bamboos. Some plants will continue to spread within containers, eventually becoming pot-bound, but if well watered and supplied with fertilizer supplements will continue to thrive. Bamboos do have one bad habit: When grown in containers they often shed leaves, but plentiful watering will often help alleviate this problem.

Water is the crucial factor. Unless you are growing a water-loving bamboo, never overwater. But also never let the roots dry out for any length of time. Use a well-drained soil mix. During active growth use a high-nitrogen fertilizer, but at half the amount suggested on the label. Provide at least a few hours of sun a day, remembering that the pots can go outdoors in the summer.

A bamboo grove in Marie Selby Botanical Garden in Florida.

General Planting Suggestions

Bamboos do well in a good organic soil with lots of added humus. They also like moisture but do not appreciate having their roots wet. When planting bamboos I dig a hole twice the size of the plant's root ball diameter and about one and a half times the root ball depth. I use a general soil mix of two parts topsoil, one part of composted manure (cow or sheep will do), and an additional one part of humus or compost.

Pleioblastus pygmaeus

Controlling Bamboo

While the stories of bamboo being used in World War II to torture prisoners by tying a victim flat on the ground, then waiting for a bamboo shoot to grow straight up into his back, are apocryphal, the news of its ability to spread are not!

Here are a few ways to contain bamboos:

- Bamboos that need light will not move into a darker area.
- Grow the bamboos so the runners amble out into an open area where they can be mowed or cut. In the same way, when runners move into the lawn, they can be continually cut back.
- While needing plenty of moisture, most bamboos will not grow in water or send runners into or underneath a stream. At the same time, bamboos will move in the direction of water, not away from water.

Mow or cut off bamboo runners that grow out of bounds.

Bamboo runners are persistent. Make sure any containment barrier is set to at least a three-foot depth and that the collar extends above ground at least three inches. Do a field check every fall, looking for runners that have gone over the collar. In the Southeast, a polyethylene barrier for bamboo should be at least eighty millimeters thick.

Propagation

There are only two ways to propagate bamboo, by dividing existing plants and by seed. Bamboos will not root from cuttings, hence the expense of buying many of the species and cultivars.

A Few Bamboo Favorites

To launch into the world of bamboos is both a pleasure and a pain: a pleasure because of the beautiful plants, and a pain dealing with the name changes as plant science marches on. The following bamboos are listed with their correct scientific names, as of 2003.

Bambusa contains various tropical bamboos with few in cultivation. Some are trees and some are shrubs, and the genus includes the large timber bamboos used to make scaffolding in eastern countries. The name *Bambusa* is from *babbu*, the Malayan name for these plants. These bamboos are clumpers. I consider three cultivars to be fine plants.

Bambusa multiplex 'Alphonse Karr' is one of the hardiest subtropicals around and the best for mountain areas in the Southeast where winters are cold. This bamboo has yellow culms vertically striped with green while the new shoots and culms are tinged with pink. In containers the usual height is about twelve feet to fifteen feet, while in the garden proper, height can be up to thirty-five feet. This bamboo will also adapt to an interior spot as long as it gets a lot of light and enough water. *Bambusa* generally makes a very tight clump, and 'Alphonse Karr' is no exception. In China, the parent species, B. *multiplex*, is used for timbers in low-cost housing and for paper pulp. Zones 8 to 10.

Alphonse Karr, born Jean Baptiste Alphonse Karr (1808–1890), was a French critic, a well-received novelist, and a brilliant journalist who became editor of *Le Figaro*. There his epigrams were frequently quoted, including *"plus ca change, plus c'est la même chose,"* or "the more things change the more they stay the same." In 1855 he went to live in Nice, where he began a career in floriculture, giving his name to this bamboo.

Bambusa multiplex 'Green Alphonse Karr' is another beauty with the stripes running in reverse, that is, green culms vertically striped with yellow. The green color is enhanced in a partial shade location. Sun. Zones 8 to 10.

Bambusa multiplex 'Fernleaf', the fernleaf bamboo, has miniature leaves measuring about a fourth of an inch by an inch and a half, growing together in fern-like rows on a six-foot plant. The plants need plenty of water to hold the foliage but may be enjoyed indoors in cool, bright rooms for long periods. Originally from China, they were used in the 1993 Los Angeles Convention Center where they grew under 150 foot-candles of light. Sun. Zones 8 to 10.

***

Otatea acuminata, the Mexican weeping bamboo, comes from the hot and humid lowlands of the state of Veracruz in Mexico. It's an elegant plant with arching stems up to ten feet long with narrow, bright green, three to six inch leaves. It is commonly called *otate* in Mexico (hence the scientific name, with the species describing the tapered leaves) and *cana brava* in Colombia. The branches are used as house rafters, particularly because they're rumored to be resistant to rotting and insect attack. (Legend has it that for the best resistance, the bamboos must be cut by the light of the full moon.)

According to Hermine Stover of Endangered Species in California, all plants from the original California clone of this bamboo flowered, and many died. From these have come thousands of seedlings and a chance to make new selections. 'Chica' is a dwarf clone with many slender stems from the base and small, very narrow leaves. It should be ideal for small tubs, while the typical form is an elegant plant for larger containers.

These clump-forming bamboos can reach a height of twenty to twenty-five feet and a spread roughly the same. They are also elegant plants for containers. Plant in full sun to light shade. Unlike many bamboos, this genus is somewhat drought tolerant when established. Zones 10a to 11.

***

Phyllostachys nigra

Phyllostachys nigra, the black bamboo, is so called because the culms are a beautiful ebony black. Each spring new canes emerge bright green, but as the summer advances, they turn to dark gray, then finally that gleaming ebony color. The generic name is from *phyllon*, "leaf," and *stachys*, "spike," referring to the growth of the stems. The leaves are four to five inches in length. Plants eventually form a grove but in this case a non-threatening grove. Eventually, the culms can reach a height of eighteen feet, but usually stay much shorter. Prefers sun to partial shade. Zones 6 to 9. Will grow in Zone 10 but is not at its best.

***

Pleioblastus is a genus containing three of my garden favorites. Once they were all in other generic categories but now reside in the genus

Pleioblastus (and here's hoping they remain in that nomenclatural niche). The generic name is from the Greek *pleios*, or "many," and *blastos*, or "buds," referring to the many branches that occur at each node.

Pleioblastus fortunei

Pleioblastus fortunei [*Pleioblastus variegatus*], or the dwarf white-stripe bamboo, bears its green leaves boldly striped with cream and green. While the compact root system usually stays put, this species can spread. Originally introduced by Robert Fortune (1812-1880), this bamboo reached England by 1876, one of the hundreds of new plants brought back from China and the Orient; Fortune also introduced to Europe the techniques involved in the art of bonsai. As with many ground-cover bamboos, this species looks better after an annual trimming. Zones 7 to 11.

Pleioblastus pygmaeus

Pleioblastus pygmaeus [*Arundinaria pygmaea*; *Sasa pygmaea*], the pygmy bamboo, is one of the smallest bamboos, with very narrow, small leaves

Pleioblastus fortunei

that, in addition to being a great (though invasive) ground cover, does wonderfully well living in a pot. When used as a ground cover it responds to getting an annual trim. It's evergreen in the Southeast, except in the higher mountains of western North Carolina. In spring, remember to remove dead culms after new growth begins. Plants can be mowed to the ground every three years to restore their good looks. Zones 5 to 10.

Pleioblastus viridistriatus

Pleioblastus viridistriatus

Pleioblastus viridistriatus [*Arundinaria viridistriata*], or the Kamuro-zasa bamboo, is a true beauty and one of a trio of garden stars. The leaves are difficult to describe—the color often depends on the time of day and the heat of the summer (colors seem to fade when summer temperatures go into the high 80s). But they have a velvety look when new, and sport varying stripes of light green (chartreuse?), plus golden tones that meld together from a distance. In the South they really need some shade, and while they are not fussy as to soil, need adequate water. The usually thirty-inch-high culms should be cut down to ground level in early spring so new growth appears. Occasionally, culms will put forth all-yellow leaves that, if propagated, result in the cultivar 'Crysophyllus'. Zones 5 to 8.

Sasa veitchii

Sasa veitchii, the Kuma bamboo grass, probably ranks as my number one bamboo for both home and garden. Because of its late autumn leaf color it's sometimes called a variegated bamboo, but it really isn't. True, the green leaves develop a light tan to off-white edge when cold weather appears, but it's just dead tissue and not a true color variation. This plant continues to be stunning in the garden until the previous year's leaves drop off in midsummer. From then to late fall it's an acceptable bamboo, but it shines in the winter garden whether planted directly outdoors or in a pot upon the terrace. The generic name is from the Japanese name for dwarf bamboos. A slow spreader, there is a smaller variety known as 'Nana' or 'Minor' that stays about three feet tall. Zones 6 to 9.

Sasella masamuniana 'Albostriata' entered my garden about six years ago, planted in the shade of a grove of hemlocks (*Tsuga canadensis*) and an umbrella magnolia (*Magnolia tripetala*). Today it has turned into a lovely grove of culms, each about five feet tall, and bearing an unbelievable variety of stunning white and green variegations. The generic name means "little sasa" (referring to the bamboo genus *Sasa*).

I have had a plant living in a rounded, handmade clay pot (about a foot wide and a foot high) for two years now. Here in my Asheville garden it winters outdoors, against the side of the house, where it's protected from chill winds and occasional snows. New leaves emerge in early spring. When frost danger is past, this bamboo spends the summer on the edge of a stone wall. It never begs for water; when I'm away, I place about a third of a new kerosene lamp wick in the soil and the rest in a nearby glass of water. Another cultivar called 'Aureostriata' has leaves dashed with yellow that fades as summer temperatures rise, about one foot tall with muted cream variegation. A treasure of subtle elegance, and particularly good indoors. I kept one in an inch-high bonsai tray for several years. In the garden it has survived in Zone 4, but is generally better in Zones 5 to 9.

Sasella masamuniana 'Albostriata'

Bamboo in Containers

Want to try your hand at bamboo bonsai or simply modify the size of your plants? I called Albert H. Adelman at Burt Associates Bamboo and asked about controlling the size of containerized bamboos.

"You can control the growth of any species by removing unwanted culms, cutting at soil level, cutting above a node, or root pruning," said Adelman. "I've kept a *Sasella masamuniana* 'Albostriata' at about a three-inch height, at home in a shallow bonsai container, for three years by cutting the culms at the nodes and feeding sparingly.

"Shorten a bamboo by cutting just above a node. While many plants look butchered if their tops are cut off, a 'topped' bamboo usually holds its looks if the remaining topmost branch is left on the side where the culm is leaning. Some bamboos, particularly *Phyllostachys* in pots, also look best, and mimic greater age, if the bottom third of the culm is bare of branches. Simply cut them off close to the culm. Also, shorten the branches of potted *Phyllostachys* to the second node of each branch. You'll get a spare look to the plant and expose and emphasize the culm. This technique is particularly effective if the culm has an interesting color or shape—and it emphasizes that bamboo quality. But if you prefer a shrubby look, don't prune the branches.

"You can dwarf a bamboo simply by restricting its growth, by growing it in the container. If fertilized, it will eventually completely fill a pot with root and rhizome. As with other bonsai, the stress of removing the plant from the container, removing some roots, and replacing the soil will restrict the growth. Remove about one-third of the roots."

Adelman went on to explain the growth process of a bamboo culm, saying that the length of a growing culm is biologically controlled at the base of the sheath that covers the culm. "A classic method of interfering with elongation and shortening a culm is to remove the culm sheath. As a result, not only is the internode shortened but it bulges a bit, giving a 'bellied' effect.

"Removing part of the culm sheath can also result in twists and turns. But be warned that this is difficult to do without destroying the culm. Culms are very soft and tender at this time and easily damaged.

"Carefully cut the culm sheaths into sections or strips. Then remove the strips over the course of a day, removing no more than one sheath a day. One sheath every other day is better yet, as the procedure imposes considerable stress on the culm. Hurry it too much and you lose the culm. I use a tool called a Clip-it (used to cut clippings out of newspapers) for the delicate job of cutting the sheaths into strips. This technique is useful only if the culm is larger than about a fourth of an inch in diameter. Or if you have a touch considerably more delicate than mine.

"With few exceptions bamboos are not difficult," Adelman said. "I treasured a nine-foot high black bamboo (*Phylostachys nigra*) grown in a pot eleven inches wide and seven inches deep. It overwintered in our house, not a greenhouse, and sat on a patio in warm weather. It took three years to get to nine-feet from a plant in a six-inch pot."

The following bamboos respond to containers with ease. Many more can be found at Adelman's firm, Burt Associates Bamboo at www.bamboos.com.

***Bambusa multiplex* 'Alophonse Karr'** is a semi-tropical clumping bamboo with yellow culms sporting vertical green stripes. Outside it's hardy to 15° F, reaching a height of up to thirty feet. Indoors near a sunny window, its height stays at about ten feet.

***Bambusa multiplex* 'Whitestripe'** is another semi-tropical clumper that bears green culms with occasional white stripes on the culms and on the leaves. Outside it's hardy to 15° F, reaching a height of thirty feet. Indoors with bright light, it will stay about ten feet high.

The marbled bamboo, **Chimonobambusa marmorea**, has marbled culms that are an attractive red color. Maximum height is six feet.

The square bamboo, **Chimonobambusa quadrangularis**, is named for the mature culms that are square rather than round. The branches and leaves drape in a beautiful manner. Adelman notes it's an excellent houseplant, reaching a height of twenty-five feet.

Chusquea coronalis, called the most beautiful bamboo in cultivation by the American Bamboo Society, is a semi-tropical clumper from Central America. Arching culms bear tiny leaves on branchlets that encircle the graceful branches. Maximum height is twenty feet outdoors but only six to eight feet in a container.

Hibanobambusa tranquillans 'Shiroshima' is a running bamboo with large, striking, variegated leaves in white and cream, reaching an indoor height of about sixteen feet.

Phyllostachys nigra, black bamboo, has shiny black culms about an inch thick and narrow green leaves up to four inches long. It's one beautiful bamboo. Outside, it's hardy to Zone 7, and while reasonably at home in a smaller pot (about eight inches across), plants do best in large tubs or containers.

Pleioblastus chino murakamianus is a small-leaved bamboo that reaches a four-foot height with leaves that show variable variegation, with some being all white.

The dwarf fern-leaf bamboo, **Pleioblastus distichus**, is hardy outside to Zone 7. This is a small, slow runner or ground cover less than three feet high, with six-inch-long, bright green leaves on culms with purplish tints.

Pleioblastus pygmaeus [*Arundinaria pygmaea*], pygmy bamboo, (Zone 7) is one of the smallest of bamboos, making an excellent garden ground cover (you can cut it with a mower if it gets out of bounds), and very much at home in a pot. It likes full sun and a moist, well-drained soil. Height is usually less than ten inches. The variegated pygmy bamboo (*P. pygmaeus* 'Variegated') has cream and white striped leaves and, because of the variegations, can take a location with open shade. Height is less than sixteen inches.

Pleioblastus shibuyanus 'Tsuboi' is a small (two- to three-feet) bamboo with unique variegation: The leaf's mid-vein is always white.

The dwarf white-stripe bamboo, **Pleioblastus variegatus**, bears green leaves with stark white variegations at a height of three feet. In the North it loses its leaves in the winter.

Pleioblastus distichus

PLANTS THAT LOOK LIKE GRASSES

At first glance some plants look exactly like members of the grass family—and at second glance, too. Their uncanny resemblance to the grasses is traced to the leaves, not the flowers. In many cases, until a close examination is performed, a plant such as black mondo grass (*Ophiopogon planiscapus*) looks exactly like a black (or dark purple) bladed grass, instead of a member of the lily family. And gardeners are easily fooled by the foliage of the willow-leaved sunflower (*Helianthus salicifolius*) never realizing, until blooming time, that it's a tall-blooming sunflower rather than a rangy grass. The following is a perfect sampling of grass look-a-likes and great places to use their particular attributes.

Lily turf (left) in the lily family, looks remarkably similar to the sedges (right).

Acorus calamus, also known as sweet flag, myrtle flag, beewort, or sometimes flagroot, is an example of the old plant adage that the more uses a species has, the more common names it will possess. In addition to the previous monikers, this herb is also called myrtle-grass, sedge-cane, sea-sedge, and sedge-root. Part of the reason for all these names lies in its value as a source of the drug calamus. The scientific name is derived from the Greek *akoras*, the classic name for the plant, in turn derived from the word *kalamos*, or "reed." The species name refers to the drug.

Sweet flag is not a grass or sedge or, for that matter, a flag, which is an iris. It is instead a member of the arum or philodendron family and while native from Nova Scotia to Ontario and south to Louisiana and Kansas, it's also found in Europe and Asia.

Calamus imparts a pleasant scent to all parts of the plant and when crushed in the fingers and tasted, yields a pungent, yet bitter taste. In early Greece the chemical was used for diseases of the eye and supposedly sailors would chew the root to relieve flatulence and toothache (a deadly combination). According to Steven Foster and James A. Duke in *A Field Guide to Medicinal Plants*, calamus has seen use as an aromatic bitter, anticonvulsant, aphrodisiac, and aid to distressed stomachs; to treat gas and heartburn; lower fevers; and relieve colds and coughs. And German studies

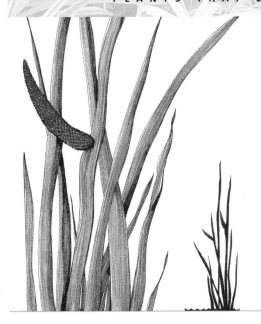

Acorus calamus

show that for maximum efficacy and safety against spasms, the diploid, or American, strains of the plant, which are devoid of beta-asarone, should be used. Plant vapors are said to repel insects, and we still haven't mentioned its uses in perfumes, cosmetics, and, in a voice from the past, one of the ingredients in Wildroot Creme Oil—Charlie!

Tracking down the spread of this plant is a classic detective story: In 1557 a Flemish diplomat for Emperor Ferdinand I first introduced the plant to European gardeners. By the end of the sixteenth century, sweet flag was growing in most European gardens and by the 1700s made its way to America. In its Asian habitat sweet flag flowers and bears fruit, but the plant that the diplomat brought to Europe doesn't flower and so never sets fruit. As a result, none of the plants brought from Europe to eastern America by most settlers ever fruited. Thus, many cultivars offered today never flower,

though some collected in the wild do. The sword-like leaves on the usual cultivars can reach a six-foot height and if in bloom they produce yellow-green spathes that arise in the mid-section of a leaf, jutting out at a ninety-degree angle.

Sweet flag is a valuable addition as a ground cover in both bog and water gardens and as long as there's water available and some shade is offered in the Deep South, these plants will prosper. Propagate sweet flag by dividing the large root: This is the part that contains most of the chemical. Zones 3 to 9.

Acorus calamus 'Variegatus' bears leaves that are variegated with longitudinal, alternate stripes of green and yellow. In this cultivar the foliage is usually about four feet tall. Like the species, this does well in tubs.

Acorus calamus 'Variegatus'

Acorus gramineus 'Variegatus'

Acorus gramineus comes from China and Japan and looks a great deal like the genus proper, but lacks the chemical properties. The foliage is dark green with a fine texture, the leaves crowded at the base, usually reaching from six inches to a foot high. The flowering spathes are a light green and bloom sporadically from late spring to midsummer. The plants usually grow at the edges of ponds. Even the smallest cultivars have a sculptural look, so try a plant in a small pot, keeping the earth just damp but protecting the plant from the summer sun at noon. Provide a fertile, moist or wet soil and remember the plants need plenty of light.

Acorus gramineus 'Variegatus' is a perennial grass-like plant sporting green and creamy-white striped leaves. Plant these in masses beside ponds or along streams or as accents or ground covers. This is the most popular of all the acorus and has enjoyed good press as a houseplant for many years. The flat, tough leaves arrange themselves like miniature folding fans and are aromatic. It's marvelous as an addition to a dish garden and outdoors at the edge of a water garden. Like most variegated plants, it should have protection from hot summer sun; if too dry the leaves quickly turn brown. This plant is also susceptible to spider mites, so be on the lookout for this insidious pest.

Acorus gramineus 'Variegatus'

Acorus gramineus 'Ogon'

Acorus gramineus 'Ogon', or the golden variegated sweet flage, has semi-evergreen foliage consisting of fanned, grass-like leaves that form a clump of sweetly scented golden foliage with stripes of green and gold, usually reaching a ten-inch height.

Acorus gramineus 'Pusillus', or the dwarf sweet flag, logs in at a height of about six inches, and is great for the pool edging or even aquariums.

Today, thanks to breeders in Japan, there are other cultivars of *Acorus gramineus*. These include 'Masamune', a variety with white-striped leaves about six inches tall; 'Oborozuki', with eight-inch-high, yellow-striped foliage; 'Pusillus Minimus', sporting leaves about two inches tall; 'Pusillus Minimus Aureus' with tiny yellow leaves; and 'Yodonoyuki', bearing green leaves with a midrib of pronounced yellow.

Butomus umbellatus, or the flowering rush, is a one-species genus of plants that is aquatic in its natural habitat, and also known as grassy rushes and water gladiolus. They are perennial herbs with thick fleshy rhizomes and many small tubers, topped with two- to four-foot flat leaves of a medium green. They grow directly in wet soil, mud, or shallow water. The generic name is from *bous*, meaning "ox," and *temno*, "cut," referring to

Butomus umbellatus

the possibility of animals cutting their mouths on the sharp leaves. The roots are said to be a food crop in Asia. The inflorescence is a terminal umbel, each flower having three leaf-like bracts and three rose-colored petals (really tepals) contrasted with red anthers.

Warning: Originally imported from Asia, then England, by 1913 flowering rushes had naturalized along the St. Lawrence River in Canada. Flowering rush has since spread throughout the northern United States and southern Canada. Because it clogs waterways and displaces native plants, it's now considered an invasive plant and so should be shunned except under perfectly controlled conditions.

Chlorophytum comosum [*Anthericum comosum*], primarily called spider plant but also known as spider ivy, ribbon plant, airplane plant, and walking anthericum, was originally an African import. It is known for the large rosettes of arching fresh green leaves two to sixteen inches long and up to an inch wide, which soon produce long arching stalks rising from the plant's crown. First these stalks bloom with small white flowers, then develop tufts of leaves with aerial roots. The generic name means "green leaf" in Greek and the species name means "with much or long hair."

These are great plants for the Southern garden—a friend puts small pots of them in second-floor window boxes for the summer months, allowing them to trail over the edge—and look marvelous in large pots on the top of pillars where the cascading stems are show-stoppers.

Spider plants are easy to grow using a good soil mix containing any good potting soil, some sharp sand, and humus. As the root ball grows, move it up to larger pots. They make great

Chlorophytum comosum 'Vittatum'

houseplants; give them plenty of light when indoors. If outside, provide filtered shade because the leaves will burn in strong summer sunlight. They prefer moist warmth and dislike temperatures below 45° F. Water well but let the soil dry out between waterings. Propagation is by seed, by division, or taking the tiny stalk-end plantlets and with a bobby pin or the like, anchoring them to potting soil until they develop strong roots of their own. Zones 9 and 10. (Note: There are reports of these plants surviving a mild winter in Asheville.)

***Chlorophytum comosum* 'Variegatum'** has attractive green leaves edged in white.

***Chlorophytum comosum* 'Vittatum'** is a smaller plant, still "spidering," with narrow, recurving leaves up to eight inches long, of dark green striped with white down the middle.

Cordyline australis

Commelina virginica, or the Virginia dayflower, can be a bit weedy, but if planted in the right place it's very useful as a ground cover, especially along the sides of streams and in bog gardens. Until it blooms, it's usually thought of as a grass, with stems standing up to four feet high.

Commelina virginica

The basal leaf blades are up to eight inches long, and smaller to the top of the stem. It blooms in summer with a small, three-petaled blue flower that belies its scientific name of *Commelina*: The genus refers to the three Commelin brothers, two of which were successful botanists and the third a wastrel and cardsharp. When first named, the European and Asiatic species were more reflective of the appellation, the flowers having two pronounced petals, and a third below the center being small, white, and easily missed. Propagation is by seed or division. Zones 6 to 9.

Cordyline australis, or cabbage grass, is usually found at garden centers and "box stores" in spring where it's sold as a centerpiece or addition to pots full of geraniums and other summer annuals. Seedlings appear as clumps of exotic-looking sword-like foliage, decidedly grass-like, quickly growing more stems. By midsummer it can have dozens of leaves, up to thirty inches long. The genus is from the Greek word for "club," referring to the stout trunk, while the species name means "from the south."

Grow plants in full sun for the best growth but partial shade will do, too. While able to grow in a predominantly clay soil, good drainage is a must. If growing in a pot, plants should be fertilized every month or so during times of active growth. When plants are about five years old they will bloom with pendant stalks of hundreds of small white flowers, and soon produce many little black seeds.

If growing from seed, follow the packet instructions and, when large enough to handle, transplant to three-inch pots, then move up in pot size as needed.

If you live in the warmer parts of Zone 8 or down to Zone 9, you can protect the trees from the threat of frosts by doing what the Japanese do, pulling all the leaves together into a point then tying them with string and covering with canvas tarp. In Zones 10 and 11, if more than a year old, most will survive an occasional frost and, if really smitten, will sprout again from the roots. Several cultivars are available, with leaf colors ranging from yellow to pink, to red-veined and just red. Zones 9 to 11.

Helianthus salicifolius, or the willow-leaved sunflower, is decidedly grass-like in appearance, until it flowers with small, sparsely scattered,

Helianthus salicifolius with yellow flowers of *Hemerocallis altissima.*

yellow daisy-like blossoms—trust me, I've been growing this plant ever since finding it pictured in color, but described as "an ornamental grass."

I found the first mention in the 1975 edition of *The Personal Garden*, a marvelous book on garden design by Bernard Wolgensinger and José Daidone. In a color photo on page 46, at the left of a trellis are eight or nine stems bound together about eighteen inches off the ground and absolutely stunning.

Then I found it again in the 1964 *Garden Guide* by Ludwig Koch-Isenburg, where the author described it thusly: "The giant sunflower, *Helianthus salicifolius*, which shoots up to eight feet, can be used as a decorative 'grass' on the banks of streams and ponds. With its long, narrow, willow-like leaves (*salicifolius* means willow-leaved) it looks just like some giant grass from the tropics; but its yellow sunflowers are unimpressive."

Turns out, it's a North American perennial, up to eight or nine feet in height, with pale, willow-like leaves up to seven inches long. Provide a good, well-drained soil, in full sun with medium moisture. Propagate by seeds or division. Zones 6 to 9.

Hypoxis hirsuta, usually called stargrass, gold stargrass, or yellow stargrass, is a grass-like herb that surprises most neophyte gardeners when it blooms in the spring. The genus is from the Greek *upoxus*, or "subacid," an old name for plants with sour leaves. The stiffly haired leaves are a beautiful olive green, reaching a height of six to twelve inches. The brilliant yellow, amaryllis-like flowers are about an inch across, appearing in spring but also off-and-on through the summer.

Stargrass makes a great ground cover in full sun and thrives on an acid soil. Although plants are tufted, they soon grow together,

Hypoxis hirsuta and *Sisyrinchium angustifolium*

resembling a miniature Swiss meadow. The plants self-seed with ease. Propagation is by seed or division of offsets. Zones 5 to 10.

Liriope muscari, or lily turf—and sometimes called monkey grass—is a member of the lily family, but with grass-like leaves. Not until the blossoms appear, their stems topped with racemes of small white to lavender flowers, does one notice the difference. Then from summer to fall, the flowers develop into black berries. The genus honors Liriope, the Greek woodland nymph who was mother to Narcissus; the species is from the Greek word for "musk," referring to the floral fragrance.

The plants multiply with ease, require little care, and make excellent ground covers. Foliage is usually a dark green, but in some varieties, it's variegated (*L. muscari* 'Variegata'). Plant height is between ten and eighteen inches and this species usually grows in a clump, eventually reaching an eighteen-inch spread. In addition to being a ground cover, liriope makes a great edging plant for the border or along a walkway, and is excellent for carpeting a bank. Space plants about a foot apart, and if the planting becomes too thick, liriope is easy to dig up and divide. The only problem is an occasional attack by a fungus known as anthracnose (the same type that attacks dogwoods). Make sure that last year's leaves are cut off and removed.

A tough plant, liriope will adapt to clay, sand, or good soil, and grows in full sun to deep shade, although in Zone 10 a bit of afternoon shade never hurts. But the soil must be well drained or not wet. Maintenance is easy: Simply cut back the old leaves in early spring before new growth begins. Zones 6 to 10. The many cultivars on the market include:

Liriope muscari

Liriope muscari 'Evergreen Giant', has stiff-textured leaf blades and white flowers, reaching a two-foot height.

Liriope muscari 'Majestic', has bright white flowers and dark foliage, growing eighteen inches tall.

Liriope muscari 'Okina' or frosted monkey grass, is a beautiful plant with leaves dusted with tones of paper-white that, when mature, have green tips.

Lirope muscari 'Pee Dee Gold'

Liriope muscari 'Pee Dee Gold', has slender, vivid yellow leaves that turn to deep gold or chartreuse as they age; adapted to hot summers.

Liriope muscari 'Silvery Sunproof', has leaves banded white and yellow; withstands sunburn better than most variegated cultivars.

Liriope spicata, or creeping lily turf, grows between ten and fifteen inches tall and will spread as long as there's room. The flowers are smaller than *L. muscari*.

Liriope spicata

'Silver Dragon' has slender, highly variegated green and white leaves and lavender flowers, reaching a twelve-inch height. 'Franklin Mint' has pale lavender flower spikes above green leaves that grow to a height of fifteen inches.

Ophiopogon japonicus, or mondo grass, also called monkey grass, is a tufted, grass-like, evergreen perennial generally growing about fourteen inches high. The half-inch-wide leaves are dark green, erect to arching, and—to prove the plants are lilies and not grasses—flower with small

Ophiopogon japonicus

white blossoms in mid- to late summer. The scientific name salutes *ophis*, or "snake," and *pogon*, or "beard," probably referring to the flower spike.

Mondo grass is usually confused with liriope (*Liriope muscari*) but the leaves of mondo grass are narrower; the plants bear smaller flowers (often hidden in the leaves); and the fruits are blue, not black as found with liriope.

Mondo grass is most often used as a ground cover or for edging along streams or garden ponds. The plants are shade tolerant and short enough to emulate a lawn without needing mowing. Provide a good, moist, but well-drained garden soil. Plants growing in shade are a darker green. Propagate by division. In early spring cut back the old leaves so there is plenty of room for new growth. Zones 7 to 10.

'Aureovariegatus' and 'Variegatus' have leaves striped with white or yellow.

'Kioto', or dwarf mondo grass, only grows about four inches high. 'Nippon' is shorter still, less than four inches in height.

Ophiopogon planiscapus 'Nigra', or black mondo grass, has leaves of dark purple, so dark they can appear to be black. Six inches tall, they are excellent shade plants but, unlike the others in this group, can often be difficult to establish. Provide partial shade.

~~~~~~~~~~~~~~~~~~~~~~~~~~~~~~~~

Phormium colensoi [*P. cookianum*], the mountain flax, is one of two species of flax lily originally from New Zealand. The genus means "basket," from the Greek word *phormos*, because baskets, floor mats, sunshades, and rope are woven from the fibers of one species. In their native haunts they're often found on poorly drained and peaty areas of mixed tussock grassland, 4,500 feet up in the mountains, not far above the tree line. It's

Phormium colensoi

said that the plants re-sprout quickly after burning and, like many grasses in the United States, may increase their numbers after a forest fire.

The mountain flax bears fairly stiff leaves up to seven feet high of either a deep maroon or deep green, sometimes fading to red with age. Originally called *P. cookianum* after the famous Captain Cook (1728–79), today the plants are known as *P. colensoi* after William Colenso (1811–99), New Zealand's most famous botanist. Colenso was originally a printer from Cornwall who immigrated to the island, translated the New Testament into the Maori language, and then, with a portable printing press, distributed copies to the local inhabitants. He became a deacon, but after losing his office in 1852 for fathering an illegitimate child, he retired to a farm, but never ceased to botanize.

Phormium tenax is the second species of New Zealand hemp. *Tenax* is Latin for "touch" and "tenacious," the plant being used for weaving. Because seedling plants vary a great deal in habit, this species is responsible for various colorful and unique cultivars. The leaves are much stiffer than those of the mountain flax and can reach a length of nine feet, growing in fans on top of heavy stems, eventually attaining a height of fifteen feet. Alfred Byrd Graf, in his valuable *Exotic Plant Manual*, writes of seeing these plants growing right in the cold waters of the southern lakes in New Zealand.

The flowers of both species are dull red or yellow and stand in erect panicles. They are more interesting than beautiful. The many cultivars include 'Variegatum', with leaves striped white and creamy yellow; 'Dazzler', bearing two-inch-wide, magenta-and chocolate-striped leaves; 'Apricot Queen', with a leaf combination of yellow and cream with green stripes and red edges; and 'Bronze Baby', a dwarf flax with leaves of bronze-purple and coppery edges.

Propagation of the species is by seed or division of the cultivars. Mountain flaxes are only hardy to 20° F, but often survive colder temperatures when grown in a sheltered place and protected from icy winds. In my garden they survived two Asheville winters only to freeze to death in the third. The warmer parts of Zones 8 and 9. In really hot climates treat them as winter annuals.

Reineckea carnea

green, two-ranked leaves from eight to sixteen inches high with a fifteen-inch spread. Often confused with *Ophiopogon*, this genus bears shorter and wider leaves and comes from a slightly warmer climate. In the summer, cup-shaped pink flowers are about half an inch wide, followed by round berries that turn red when they are ripe.

Provide a moist but well-drained soil in full sun or in partial shade. For an extended dry season, keep the soil watered. To prevent crowding, lift and divide the plants every three years. Propagate by division or by seeds. Zones 9 and 10.

Reineckea carnea, or fan-grass, also answers to the name of reineckea. It's a one-of-a-kind genus, native to the warmer regions of China and Japan, found growing in grass-like clumps with shiny

Sisyrinchium angustifolium, or blue-eyed grass, is a genus name of some seventy-five species of perennial plants native to the Western Hemisphere, and, while closely resembling grasses (except in bloom), are really members of the iris family. The genus is taken from an old word used by Theophrastus for a bulbous plant.

The leaves are glaucous to dark green, stiffly upright, and fine in texture, usually growing to a length of four to eight inches. The flowers are six-petaled, varying in color from a pale blue to violet—rarely white—about half an inch wide. The round fruits appear in summer. The plants do best in full sun to partial shade, preferring a good, moist, well-drained soil. Propagation is by seed or division.

When massed in bunches, they are attractive in leaf but charming in bloom. They naturalize with ease and look great in the rock garden or the wild garden, or just gracing the border. Zones 4 to 9.

Sisyrinchium angustifolium

Sisyrinchium angustifolium 'Lucerne'

bears larger flowers—three-fourths of an inch wide—of rich blue-purple, flowering from May to July. They are eight inches tall.

Sisyrinchium palmifolium [S. macrocephalum],

the yellow-eyed grass, hails from South America and forms a twenty-inch-wide clump of evergreen blue-green leaves up to twenty inches tall. The inch-wide flowers open in late afternoon. Self-sown seedlings appear regularly around it and plants often die after a few years in the garden, but seed is plentiful. Zones 7 to 9.

Sisyrinchium tinctorium 'Puerto Yellow',

or the Mexican yellow-eyed grass, was collected by Tony Avent in Mexico in 1994. The plants grow about a foot tall and begin to flower in spring, then off and on into early summer. Three-fourth-inch, bright yellow flowers are coveted by all who see the plants in bloom. Zones 7b to 10.

Tulbaghia violacea,

or the tricolor society garlic, is a bulbous plant that is decidedly grass-like in appearance, until summer when dainty heads of lilac pink flowers rise on two-foot stalks above the blue-gray foliage that is edged with white. The generic name is in honor of Ryk Tulbach, a Dutch governor of the Cape of Good Hope where these bulbs originate. The species name reflects the violet color of the flowers. New spring growth has a pink tinge and brushing against the foot-high leaves emits a fragrance of garlic. The common name refers to a supposed fact that although the plant tastes like garlic, if ingested you won't get bad breath. Plants need at least four hours of sun a day and night temperatures should stay above 40° F. Zones 7 to 11.

Tulbaghia violacea

Typha angustifolia, the common or narrow-leaved cattail, belongs to a genus with ten species found in the temperate and tropical regions of both hemispheres. In England and Europe, cattails are known as bulrushes, a name that in America is usually reserved for horsetails and sedges. Other common names include great reed mace, nail-rod, and Cossack asparagus. The scientific name of *Typha* stands for *tuphe*, an ancient Greek name of the plant.

These are tall water-dwelling plants with stout stems and grass-like foliage, the leaves erect and blade-like, up to three-fourths of an inch wide and between three and six feet in length. The flowers are sausage-like heads of tightly packed female flowers, topped with a thin tail of staminate (male) flowers. And, except for the cultivars, cattails are very, very invasive, so care must be taken when using them, especially in a natural setting.

The uses of cattails are many: Flour can be made from the pollen, stems and leaves make

Typha latifolia

valuable thatching, the fluff is a good substitute for kapok, the thickened rootstocks make a great survival food, and the flammable pollen has been used by fireworks manufacturers. And not only is it valuable for people, it's high on the list for wildlife, too, as food, nesting material, and cover.

Cattails have a specific place to grow: They thrive in mud or in shallow water. The rootstocks should be held by a stout container, or protected from spreading with a barrier sunk to at least two feet. Plant the roots to a depth of about six inches. Heavy clay or pond mud is essential to growth. They also need full sun. Zones 5 to 9.

Typha latifolia is the largest of the cattails, with leaves from six to ten feet tall. Zones 5 to 10.

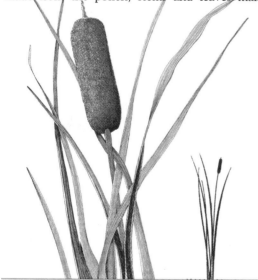

Typha angustifolia

Typha minima, or the dwarf cattail, is a small species best used in the home water garden. Introduced from Japan, it's a native of Europe and Asia. This miniature has leaves one-fourth of an inch wide and about two feet in length. The male flowers appear in summer, standing above the familiar brown "hot dog" of female flowers—only in this species, it's more like a Vienna sausage. After bloom, the male flowers rapidly disappear, leaving a naked stalk tip. Propagate by division in spring. Foliage turns yellow-brown in autumn. Fruiting spikes usually persist to early winter before disintegrating, but to dry properly they must be picked and gathered before the male flowers stop blooming. Zones 3 to 10.

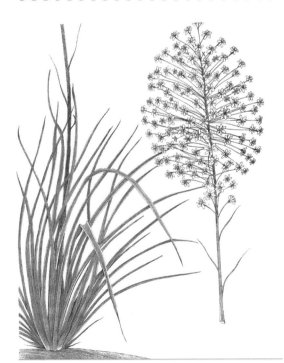

Xerophyllum asphodeloides

Xerophyllum asphodeloides [*X. setifolium*], called beargrass, turkey-beard, or mountain asphodel, is a fantastic grass-like plant that, until it sends up its many-flowered stem, looks for all the world like a beautiful and incredibly healthy, mountain grass. The genus name is from the Greek *xeros*, or "arid," and *phyllon*, for "leaf." Stems are up to four feet long and topped with light green, grass-like leaves that form dense mounds of growth—and that growth looks deceptively like a grass. They grow in the mountains around Asheville, especially on mountain summits, where the drainage is close to perfect, and the edge of bogs. I've found them growing in the mountains where the plants are buffeted by weather, in full sun, or even partial shade. Propagation is by division or by seed. Zones 5 to 9.

Xyris arenicola, or yellow-eyed grass, is represented in North America by various species. These plants are tufted herbs, basal leaves decidedly rush-like and, until they bloom, are usually taken for a rush or a grass. These fine-textured leaves are gray or bluish green, very narrow, up to sixteen inches long. The generic name is from the Greek *xyris*, a plant with two-edged leaves, a name coming from the Greek *xyron*, or "razor." The species name is Greek for "dwelling in the sand."

When flowering occurs, spirally twisted stems (or scapes) grow a little over two feet high topped with scale-like bracts, not unlike tiny pinecones, that give rise to half-inch-wide, three-petaled flowers.

While not exactly show-stopping plants in themselves, yellow-eyed grasses delight in growing and naturalizing at the edges of bogs or small pools. Propagation is by division and by seed. Zones 6 to 10.

Xyris fimbriata, yellow-eyed grass, is a larger species with leaves up to four feet high and yellow flowers (the bracts are fringed, hence the species name, from the Latin *fimbriae*, meaning "fringe"). This, too, is a plant for naturalizing in low, wet, but sandy sites. Propagation is by division and seeds. Zones 6 to 10.

Yucca filamentosa

Yucca aloifolia, the Spanish bayonet, is a native yucca that eventually forms a trunk as the lower leaves die off. The dark green foliage is stiff and pointed, up to two and a half feet long, and two inches wide with toothed margins. The species name points out that the leaves resemble those of the aloe. Eventually plants can reach a height of fifteen feet with a five-foot spread. Summer-blooming flowers are fragrant and night blooming. Provide sun or partial shade, and average soil with good drainage—sandy loam is best. This plant works at the shore and in city gardens. The only maintenance is removing dead leaves. Zones 8 and 9.

Yucca filamentosa, the common yucca, is an American native plant with a great deal of history and many uses in the garden. The most popular name for this species is Adam's needle, because the leaves come to a sharp point and the edges throw off numerous fine white hairs that are the thickness of buttonhole thread. A great number of American plants were imported into Europe during the sixteenth century, including tobacco, the potato, nasturtiums, sunflowers, and the yucca. *Yucca* is based on the Spanish *yuca*, a word for manioc (*Manihot esculenta*), a major source for the bitter cassava, the name of which is based on a Taino Indian word for this plant. Although used in error, the name stuck. The species name refers to those loose fibers on the leaf margins,

fibers used by the Indians of the Southwest as thread and in weaving cloth.

Yuccas appear to be related to grasses until midsummer, when a strong flower stem appears, shooting up higher than the surrounding leaves—often to six feet or more—and bearing numerous cream-colored, bell-like, pendant flowers. Most gardeners are familiar with these imposing plants, but few realize that the tall spires of white, summer-blooming, bell-shaped flowers are pollinated in their native desert homes by a night-flying species of moth. While not specifically night-blooming plants since the flowers are open during the day, yucca flowers exhibit nyctinasty, the art of being nyctitropic (in other words, they move at night). As darkness falls, the individual flowers perk up and point to the night sky, exuding pleasant fragrances to attract pollinating moths or sometimes bats.

Because a well-grown plant will often be over three feet in diameter, these are not for the small garden. But the plant form, plus the interesting seedpods, make yuccas valuable additions to a landscape that has the space to hold them. Use these plants with plenty of

Yucca filamentosa 'Golden Sword'

Yucca smalliana 'Bright Edge'

rocks or in groups of three or more. Gravel mulch is more in keeping with the look of the plant than leaf mulch or peat moss (always a no-no because it's either too wet or too dry).

Once established, yuccas will perform every year, regardless of the amount of rain that falls, because they have a very deep taproot.

The following are but a sampling of the yuccas available at today's nurseries.

Yucca filamentosa 'Color Guard' becomes a thirty-inch-high, thirty-inch-wide clump of leaves, green striped down the center midrib, with a wind band of yellow that turns to a creamy gold in midsummer. Zones 5 to 10.

Yucca filamentosa 'Golden Sword' grows about thirty inches tall and two feet wide, with dark green leaves with a bright yellow center. Zones 4 to 10.

Yucca filamentosa 'Variegata' bears dark, eighteen-inch, green leaves edged with creamy white. Zones 5 to 10.

Yucca gloriosa 'Variegata', or the variegated soapwort, originally came from the JC Raulston Arboretum, where the two- to three-foot-wide clumps reached a four-foot height in some ten years. The blue-green leaves are bordered with a margin that begins as a golden-yellow, then with the advance of summer's heat changes to a rich creamy white. Zones 7 to 10.

Yucca rostrata, or the beaked blue yucca, has narrow powder-blue leaves that fan out from a central stalk that with age look like a "Cousin Itt" on a stick. Tony Avent writes that in ten years the gardener can expect a four-foot trunked specimen that will branch with age. Better in alkaline soil. Zones 5 to 10.

Yucca smalliana 'Bright Edge' is best for the small garden, being about eighteen inches tall and twenty inches wide with dark green leaves edged with a wide band of creamy gold. Zones 5 to 10.

Bibliography

Arber, Agnes. *The Gramineae: A Study of Cereal, Bamboo, and Grass*. Weinheim, Germany: J. Cramer, 1965.

Bailey Hortorium. *Hortus Third: A Concise Dictionary of Plants Cultivated in the United States and Canada*. New York: The Macmillan Publishing Company, 1976.

Bell, Michael. *The Gardener's Guide to Growing Temperate Bamboos*. Portland, Oregon: Timber Press, 2000.

Bews, J. W. *The World's Grasses*. London: Longmans, Green and Co., 1929.

Bisset, Peter. *The Book of Water Gardening*. New York: A.T. De La Mare Printing and Publishing Co., Ltd., 1905.

Brown, Lauren. *Grasses: An Identification Guide*. Boston, Massachusetts: Houghton Mifflin, 1979.

Chase, Agnes. *First Book of Grasses: The Structure of Grasses Explained for Beginners*. Washington, D.C.: Smithsonian Institution Press, 1964.

Darke, Rick. *The Color Encyclopedia of Ornamental Grasses*. Portland, Oregon: Timber Press, 1999.

Earle, Alice Morse. *Old-Time Gardens*. New York: The Macmillan Company, 1901.

Fitter, Richard and Alastair Fitter. *Collins Guide to the Grasses, Sedges, Rushes, and Ferns of Britain and Northern Europe*. London: William Collins Sons & Co Ltd., 1984.

Francis, Mary Evans. *The Book of Grasses*. New York: Doubleday, Page & Company, 1912.

Foerster, Karl. *Einzug der Gräser und Farne in die Gärten*: First Edition. Melsunger: Neumann Verlag, 1957.

Gleason, Henry A., Ph.D. *The New Britton and Brown Illustrated Flora of the Northeastern United States and Adjacent Canada*. New York: Hafner Publishing Company, Inc., 1963.

Greenlee, John. *The Encyclopedia of Ornamental Grasses*. Emmaus, Pennsylvania: Rodale Press, 1992.

Grounds, Roger. *Ornamental Grasses*. Bromley, Kent, United Kingdom: Christopher Helm, 1989.

Hitchcock, A. S. *Manual of the Grasses of the United States*. New York: Dover Publications, Inc., 1971.

_____. *Manual of the Grasses of the West Indies*. Washington, D.C.: United States Government Printing Office, 1936.

Hubbard, C. E. *Grasses*. Middlesex, England: Penguin Books, 1954.

Loewer, H. Peter. *Growing and Decorating with Grasses*. New York: Walker and Company, 1977.

_____. *The Indoor Window Garden*. Chicago: Contemporary Books, 1990.

_____. *Solving Weed Problems*. Guilford, Connecticut: The Lyons Press, 2001.

_____, Editor. *Plants & Gardens: Ornamental Grasses*. Brooklyn: Brooklyn Botanic Garden, 1989.

Loewer, Peter and Lawrence Mellinchamp. *The Winter Garden: Planning and Planting for the Southeast*. Mechanicsburg, Pennsylvania, 1997.

Meyer, Mary Hockenberry. *Ornamental Grasses*. New York: Charles Scribners' Sons, 1973.

Oakes, A. J. *Ornamental Grasses and Grasslike Plants*. New York: Van Nostrand Reinhold, 1990.

Ohwi, Jisaburo. *Flora of Japan*. Washington, D.C.: Smithsonian Institution Press, 1965.

Ottesen, Carole. *Ornamental Grasses: The Amber Wave*. New York: McGraw-Hill Publishing Company, 1989.

Stearn, William T. *Botanical Latin:* Third Edition. North Pomfret, Vermont: David & Charles, 1983.

Thomas, Graham Stuart. *Perennial Garden Plants*. Third Edition. Portland, Oregon: Sagapress, Inc./Timber Press, Inc., 1990.

Plants:

Burt Associates Bamboo
P.O. Box 719-W
Westford, MA 01886
www.bamboos.com

Collector's Nursery
16804 NE 102nd Avenue
Battle Ground, WA 98604
360-574-3832
www.collectorsnursery.com

Digging Dog Nursery
P.O. Box 471
Albion, CA 95410
707-937-1130
www.diggingdog.com

Forest Farm
990 Tetherow Road
Williams, OR 97544-9599
541-846-7269
www.forestfarm.com

Glasshouse Works
Church Street, P.O. Box 97
Stewart, OH 45778-0097
740-662-2142
www.rareplants.com

Heronswood Nursery
7530 NE 288th Street
Kingston, WA 98346-9502
360-297-4172
www.heronswood.com

New England Bamboo
Company
5 Granite Street
Rockport, MA 01966
978-546-3581
www.newengbamboo.com

Niche Gardens
1111 Dawson Road
Chapel Hill, NC 27516
919-967-0078
www.nichegardens.com

Plant Delights Nursery, Inc.
9241 Sauls Road
Raleigh, NC 27603
919-772-4794
www.plantdelights.com

Plants of the Southwest
Aqua Fria, Rte 6, Box 11-A
Santa Fe, NM 87501
800-788-7333
www.plantsofthesouthwest.com

Pond-A-Rama
Bettyjean Kling
717-532-7212
www.pondarama.com

Trans-Pacific Nursery
20110 Canyon Road
Sheridan, OR 97378
www.worldplants.com

Variegated Foliage Nursery
245 Westford Road
Eastford, CT 06242
860-974-3951

The Water Garden Shop
25289 SW Stafford Road
Tualatin, OR 97062
503-638-1709
www.thewatergardenshop.com

Seeds:

Chiltern Seeds
Bortree Stile, Ulverston,
Cumbria LA12 7PB
England
www.chilternseeds.co.uk

The Fragrant Path
P.O. Box 328
Fort Calhoun, NE 68023

J. L. Hudson, Seedsman
Star Route 2, Box 337
La Honda, CA 94020
www.jlhudsonseeds.net

Park Seed Company
1 Parkton Avenue
Greenwood, SC 29647-0001
800-845-3369
www.countrysidegardens.com

Prairie Nursery
P.O. Box 306
Westfield, WI 53964
800-476-9453
www.prairienursery.com

Thompson & Morgan
P.O. Box 1308
Jackson, NJ 08527-0308
800-274-7333
www.thompson-morgan.com